WHAT EVERYONE IN BRITAIN
SHOULD KNOW ABOUT
CRIME AND PUNISHMENT

WHAT EVERYONE IN BRITAIN SHOULD KNOW ABOUT CRIME AND PUNISHMENT

David Wilson
John Ashton

BLACKSTONE PRESS LIMITED

First published in Great Britain 1998 by Blackstone Press Limited, Aldine Place, London W12 8AA. Telephone 0181-740 2277

© John Ashton, David Wilson 1998

ISBN: 1 85431 736 9

British Library Cataloguing in Publication Data
A CIP catalogue record for this book is available from the British Library

Typeset by Montage Studios Limited, Horsmonden, Kent
Printed by Ashford Colour Press, Gosport, Hampshire

Contents

9 Probation and Alternatives to Prison   139

The historical roots of probation — A changing service — The
probation service in the 1990s — *The extension of punishment in
the community — The rise of the managed service — The effect of
'law and order' politics* — Who is on probation? — Good
probation practice — *The Essex Motor Project — Birmingham
Prison's Stepping Out programme — Leeds Victim – Offender Unit*
— Probation and the future

Acknowledgements

We would like to thank the following people: Barbara McCalla, who typed much of the manuscript; Judy Timms and Ros Holt, who also helped with the typing; Tamsen Courtenay who helped with the copying; the Prison Reform Trust for allowing us to use their excellent library and research facilities, and especially Stephen Shaw and Stephen Nathan; UCE for allowing us to use their facilities for the first two of our committee meetings, and the New Bridge who gave us the use of their boardroom for the third; the Directors and staff of Just TV; Danny Rosenbaum; Celia Ellis and Rachel Ashton and Leslie and Lois Clifton; Peter Gartside; Alison, Anne and Margaret Wilson; Peter Lee-Wright; Frank Cook; Erik Skon; everyone at Blackstone Press; and, last but never least, Anne Maguire.

In particular we would like to thank our committee (see Appendix), who guided our reading and gave us encouragement at every stage in the production of the book.

List of Tables and Figures

Introduction

Together the police, courts, probation and prison services make up what is called our criminal justice system. It is their job to tackle crime and punish those who offend against us. That is their role and their responsibility, and as such our criminal justice system is a complete failure. If your gas central heating system worked like our criminal justice system, you would have long ago had to switch to oil, or you would have frozen to death.

We argue that while it retains a symbolic importance, the criminal justice system plays only a very minor part in controlling the incidence and seriousness of crime, despite what is claimed by politicians and by those who work within the system. The criminal justice system has consistently failed to satisfy public expectations and will continue to do so; and thus the fear of crime will continue to dominate conversations in our homes, in the pub, and in the street. This in turn will lead to increasingly urgent calls for politicians of all parties to 'take action' and, often prompted by the media, in the face of contradictory evidence, short-term solutions will be grasped from thin air in the hope of doing something about crime. One by one, each of these still-born initiatives thereafter will be forgotten and quietly dropped.

Prison in particular has played a central role within the criminal justice system, and our prison population has as a consequence increased dramatically. In July 1992 the prison population of England and Wales was 47,000. Five years later it was 63,000, a level which recent official predictions suggested would not be reached until the year

2004, and which has forced the prison service to house prisoners in a converted ship and investigate the use of holiday camps as prisons. Indeed the prison population increased by 10,000 between 1995 and 1997. With the passage of the Crime (Sentences) Act 1997, which had the broad support of both the Conservative and Labour parties, American-style legislation has been introduced covering such matters as mandatory minimum sentences, which will undoubtedly increase the prison population still further and effectively end parole as it is currently understood. This is no small matter, for as Home Office research itself indicates, parolees re-offend less often than those not granted parole, and the offences which they do commit are less serious.

The cost of all this is horrendous. Expenditure in 1993/94 for the whole of the criminal justice system was £9,424m, slightly less than was spent on the transport system of the country as a whole, and more than double that which was spent on employment. Most of this money went to the police, who had a budget of £6,022m, representing a 41 per cent increase in real terms since 1986/87. Expenditure on the prison service reached £1,509m in the same year, which was an increase in real terms of 46 per cent from 1986/87. The vast majority of these budgets went to pay staff costs, which in relation to the prison service amounted to two-thirds of total operating costs. On average it costs £2,000 per month to keep an adult male offender in custody in 1994. The probation service is the poor relation of the criminal justice system and received only £488m, despite the fact that a community service order cost the taxpayer only £100 per month to maintain, which at the very least represents value for money. However, government spending on crime prevention was even less, and spread between the Department of Environment, the Home Office, and the Welsh Office etc., amounted to some £240m, or 2.5 per cent of the total system's budget.

It is not necessary to continue like this, but we need to stop now and fundamentally re-assess our nation's priorities in relation to crime and punishment. Our view is that with greater emphasis on crime prevention, rather than the current obsession over what to do with an offender when a crime has been committed, and the perpetrator detected and convicted, the prison population would be significantly reduced, and new and more imaginative roles would evolve for the police and probation service. Already positive — but local — policing and probation initiatives successfully divert those who have offended or who are at risk of offending, away from crime, which serves the public both in relation to cost and in making communities safer.

These initiatives cannot succeed in isolation. They need help and support from others in our community if we are truly to tackle the causes of crime. In particular, we believe that as a quarter of all known offenders are under 18, schools must play a more prominent role in crime prevention, and that they must be appropriately resourced to do so. Quite simply, spending money in our schools now reduces the need to spend a great deal more on prisons in the future. This lesson is particularly apparent in California, where the 'three strikes' laws and 'truth in sentencing' initiatives are estimated to cost $4.5–6.5 billion per year to implement. This money has to be found from somewhere, and in 1996 state expenditure on prisons increased by over 13 per cent, which was more than twice the increase for education. Indeed, in 1980 California spent 3 per cent of the state budget on prisons, and 10 per cent on higher education. By 1994 the state was spending 8 per cent on prisons, and 8 per cent on higher education. If we do not want a similar picture to emerge here, we need to act now.

The need for urgency is obvious, as the picture emerging in our own country does not give us too much confidence. Indeed, the knowledge that permanent school exclusions are now at an all-time high is particularly worrying. In 1995/1996 there were over 10,000 permanent school exlusions in England and Wales, and in 1997 nearly 1 million children, or 1 in 8 of the school-age population, missed at least one half day's schooling without permission. Yet we know that 70 per cent of young offenders are either regular truants, or have been excluded from school. In short, the link between educational failure and crime is plain for all to see, but the introduction of school 'league tables' seems to prevent people from moving forward on this issue. We will draw attention to good schools practice, which shows how some schools cope with difficult pupils without damaging the standards of others. Ironically, in February 1998, the Home Secretary announced a special 'booster package' of £70m for HM Prison Service to help it cope with the growing prison population, just a few days after New Labour had announced — with great fanfare — a much lower budget to reduce class sizes in our primary schools. Is this not evidence enough that we've got out priorities wrong?

Similarly, better housing, enhanced work skills and opportunities reduce the amount and seriousness of crime in our community. These simple facts underline the importance of properly resourcing our communities in relation to a range of initiatives, from transport policies and concierges in tower blocks, to recreational facilities for young people and better street lighting. However, the various departments of government rarely seem to act in concert; the different components of the criminal justice system too often believing that they are in competition with each other, preventing real progress from taking place. As a result our agenda on these matters is too often set by the tabloid media, scaring the public into having politicians take action against, for example, such threats as dangerous dogs and beggars in the streets.

Real progress on these issues cannot take place until the public's fear of crime is acknowledged and addressed, rather than simply being manipulated to sell newspapers, TV programmes, or for electoral benefit. Too often the public's fear of crime does not relate to the factual position. For example, most people believe that the vast majority of crime in England and Wales is violent. In fact, in 1997, 91 per cent of recorded crimes were property offences, including burglary, theft, and criminal damage. Only 8 per cent of recorded crimes were crimes of violence, including sexual offences. Of the 350,698 crimes of violence recorded by the police in 1997, 72 per cent related to minor woundings, and only 0.2 per cent to murder and manslaughter. Significantly, these very serious crimes are the ones which are cleared up most regularly by the police. For example, 91 per cent of all murders were cleared up in 1997. The reason for this is not to difficult too determine. Despite what we see in our newspapers, or watch on our TVs, the vast majority of murders happen within the extended family. As a result, you do not need Inspectors Morse, Taggart, Dalgleish, Tennyson, or Dalziel to work out 'who did it', as simple statistics will indicate that it is the husband, or wife, or lover, or brother or sister, or son or daughter. This is not to underestimate the problem, as some of our communities do indeed suffer from high levels of violent crime and vandalism, but the solutions to these problems rarely lie within the criminal justice system.

In particular we believe that the central role in policy accorded to imprisonment should be replaced with a greater emphasis on community penalties, particularly those with a reparative or restorative element. Prison should only ever be used as a last resort, and when no alternative method of punishment is appropriate. When people are incarcerated, the prison should provide all possible opportunities to help the prisoner lead a crime-free life on release. We believe that several prisons in our country provide positive examples of what can be done to help offenders, and that we should learn in particular from the lessons of such prisons as HMP Grendon — one of the few in Europe which operates as a therapeutic community.

We also deal with one of the biggest causes of 'crime' in Britain today — drugs. In doing so we attempt to present the realities of drug-taking in Britain, which as the Home Secretary discovered, is widespread. We argue, on the basis of a variety of evidence and research, for a less punitive approach to this issue. In doing so, we will describe the total failure of the mandatory drug testing programme in our prisons. If we can't stop drug trafficking into our prisons, how on earth can we succeed within the community as a whole?

This book stems from frustration: a frustration born of successive Conservative Governments who ultimately proceeded on the basis that 'prison works' when regime conditions were at their most basic, and of a new Labour Government which seems to want to expand, rather than reduce, the role of the criminal justice system; a frustration born of the knowledge of the realities of crime and punishment, rather than the steady stream of sensationalism and myth; a frustration born of the ever-increasing costs of the criminal justice system, with very little return for our money; and lastly a frustration born of the fear of the type of society we will become if we continue to police our country in the way in which we have, and to incarcerate at the rate at which we do. How long will this state of affairs continue until we become 'Gulag Britain'?

This book is a collaborative effort (an Appendix of those who advised the authors is attached). While not written by a committee, the book could not have been completed without the guidance and advice of a variety of experts who worked with the authors. These range from police officers and a barrister, to prison governors; from ex-offenders, to a politician and members of the public; from teachers and academics, to probation officers and charity workers. All bring to this debate the same sense of frustration about crime and punishment in this country, and a common desire to do something about it. We hope that through this book we will stimulate debate; not amongst criminologists and criminal justice practitioners but amongst the 'man and woman in the street'. In doing so we hope that they too will share our sense of frustration, and correspondingly encourage others to take action.

1 Crime in Britain

What proportion of British men over 40 have a criminal record? One in 20 perhaps, or one in 10? In fact the answer is one in three,[1] a figure which is all the more staggering when one takes into account that it excludes motoring offences. Clearly a third of the adult population are not a menace to society, yet there is a general perception that Britain has a substantial crime problem which has grown steadily worse.

So how bad have things got? This chapter will attempt to answer this question, and in doing so will demonstrate that the issue is not as straightforward as it might at first appear. It will also address the still more complicated issue of what causes crime. Lastly, it will set the context for the later chapters by describing the failed attempts of recent governments to tackle the crime problem and by examining the approach of the New Labour Government.

THE CRIME PROBLEM

A problem of definition

Crime does not exist as a fixed entity. It is not a 'thing' out there, somewhere in Britain, waiting to be discovered, for politicians to condemn and the police to put a stop to. When we think of crime we

---

[1] *Sunday Times* article, 'A Nation of Thieves', 11 January 1998.

think of burglary, auto theft, robbery, assault, murder; but crime is constantly evolving and developing. Behaviour which previously was seen as 'criminal' can become lawful, such as consenting homosexual behaviour between 18-year-olds. Equally, previously legal activities, such as not wearing a seat-belt in a car or a crash helmet on a motorbike, have become illegal.

The 1980s and 1990s have, in particular, seen new crimes invented for specific groups or behaviour associated with those groups, targetted by successive governments. For example, laws have been passed against joyriders, squatters, hunt saboteurs, and New Age travellers. Similarly, the Teddy Boys of the 1950s, the Mods and Rockers of the 1960s, the Punks of the 1970s, can all be linked to the youth culture of raves and acid house of the late-1980s and early-1990s in that they have all attracted censure and hostility. This can sometimes lead to criminalisation, and so, for example, the possession of the drug 'ecstasy' is now illegal. This process is not simply confined to the activities of people, as the owners of 'dangerous dogs' will testify.

All of this makes some of the certainties about crime of which we have been assured more difficult to sustain. If crimes can be abolished or invented, how can we tell if crime in our country is getting better or worse? How can we tell if crime is rising or falling if it is impossible to find an accurate definition of what it is that we are attempting to measure?

Not only are there problems in accurately defining 'crime', but measuring it is also a problem. No less a figure than the editor of the Home Office's official digest of information on the criminal justice system, for example, commented that 'no one knows the true extent of crime in this country. Two main measures are available but each, in its own way, may not accurately record the scale of crime.'[2]

The first of these two main measures is the official crime figures recorded by the police. These are flawed because, for a variety of reasons, some crimes go unreported. For example, victims might regard the crimes committed against them as too trivial to report, or believe that they might not be treated sympathetically or seriously by the police. Other crimes such as tax evasion (which is recorded by the Inland Revenue) or VAT evasion (which is recorded by Customs and Excise)

---

[2] *Digest: Information on the Criminal Justice System in England and Wales*, Home Office: Research and Statistics Department, 1995, p. 1.

will appear in official criminal statistics only if the perpetrator is subsequently brought to court. It could be argued that the economic damage created by these offences is far more damaging than those offences against property which make up the bulk of our official statistics, and yet it is rare for them to appear in official accounts of crime in our country.

Alternatively, the increase in crime so graphically displayed in Table 1 (below) might also reflect merely an increased reporting of crime. For example, a nationwide anti-burglary campaign was mounted in 1982, partly in response to a 50 per cent increase in the number of recorded burglaries between 1971 and 1981. Yet information from other sources suggests that there was almost no change in the rate of burglary at all, and that the increase in the amount of reported and subsequent recording of burglary can be accounted for by the greater availability of 'new for old' insurance policies, which produced an incentive for increased claims.[3]

---

[3] K. Bottomley and K. Pease, *Crime and Punishment: Interpreting the Data*, Milton Keynes: Open University Press, 1986.

Source: Information on the Criminal Justice System in England and Wales, Home Office 1993, plus update.

Table 1: Crimes recorded in England and Wales, 1876–1996

Other factors might also effect the extent of recorded crime. For example, the number of reported incidents of criminal damage shot up from 17,000 in 1969 to 124,000 in 1977. Criminal damage is officially defined as damage exceeding £20.00 in value, so the 'increase' could have been largely due to inflation moving trivial incidents of damage into a more serious category of crime, rather than to an increased level of vandalism.[4]

The other main measure of crime, besides the figures recorded by the police, is the British Crime Survey (BCS). First conducted in 1982, the BCS is in effect a victim survey conducted by the Home Office on a random sample of the population aged 16 and over, about offences they have experienced in the previous year. Because it includes those crimes not reported to the police, as well as those which are, it is generally seen as providing a more accurate picture of the extent of crime in this country, and can therefore be used in comparison to the official statistics mentioned above to reveal what is known as 'hidden crime', or crime which does not get recorded. This often paints a picture at odds with that drawn by the use of other statistical measures of crime by revealing, for example, that people from ethnic minorities are more likely to be the victims, rather than the perpetrators, of crime.

Yet the BCS also has its critics, especially as the evidence it reveals is often used to confirm rather than confound the popular assumptions about the nature and extent of crime in this country (see below). Nor do surveys such as the BCS tell us anything about corporate crimes as perpetrated by Robert Maxwell, Peter Clowes or Asil Nadir, or of the theft of an estimated $10m by the directors of the Bank of Commerce and Credit International.[5]

A growing problem

For all the difficulties there are in accurately defining and measuring crime, all the indications are that Britain's crime problem has grown steadily. The levels of recorded crime in England and Wales, notwithstanding the occasional annual fall, have risen almost since records began [See Table 1].

Over the last two decades the rises have been especially sharp. In 1979 there were around 2.4 million crimes recorded in England and

---

[4] *The New Statesman*, 22 January 1982.

[5] Figures taken from the *Guardian* (2), 1 July 1993.

Wales, but by 1992 that figure had reached over 5.4 million. From 1994 onwards there were annual falls, and by 1997 the figure was 4.6 million. As we will see in Chapter 3, in any one year only around 6 per cent of crimes are violent, and only a small proportion of those involve serious violence. Vehicle crimes make up about 28 per cent of the total, burglary 24 per cent, and other theft 23 per cent.[6]

Since it began in 1982, the BCS has largely painted a far bleaker picture than have the recorded crime figures. Each of the six surveys has suggested that at most only half of known crime is reported, a figure which has progressively shrunk and may be as low as a quarter.[7] The 1996 International Crime Victimisation Survey contained more bad news. Based on interviews with 20,000 people in 11 countries, it found that around 31 per cent of British respondents had been victims of crime in the past 12 months, a figure matched only by The Netherlands. England and Wales, along with the US, at around 3.5 per cent, also had the highest rate of contact crimes, such as robbery and assault.[8] [see Table 2].

Official statistics reveal some other trends about crime in Britain. For example, they indicate that criminal activity is predominantly the preserve of men and that the peak age of offending is 18 for men, and 15 for women.

There are marked patterns among victims as well as offenders. Home Office research found that in 1992, 14 per cent of the population reported 71 per cent of all incidents. A study of the crime statistics for 1984, 1988 and 1992 revealed that 4 per cent of victims suffered 44 per cent of crimes.[9]

The statistics recording the rate at which police forces catch criminals — the so-called clear-up rate — also make depressing reading. In 1980, the clear-up rate for England and Wales was 40 per cent, but by 1994 it had fallen to less than 25 per cent.[10] Thankfully the clear-up rate for serious violent offences has always been considerably higher. In 1997

---

[6] 1992 figures cited in the *Independent*, 29 April 1993.

[7] J. Muncie (1996), 'The Construction and Deconstruction of Crime', in J. Muncie and E. McLaughlin (eds) *The Problem of Crime*, London: Sage, pp. 22-3.

[8] *Criminal Victimisation in Eleven Industrialised Countries: Key Findings from the 1996 International Crime Victimisation Survey*, prepared for the EU Conference 14 May 1997.

[9] 'Growing minority suffering bulk of crime, say researchers', the *Guardian*, 29 March 1995.

[10] Police force survey carried out by the *Guardian*, 31 January 1994.

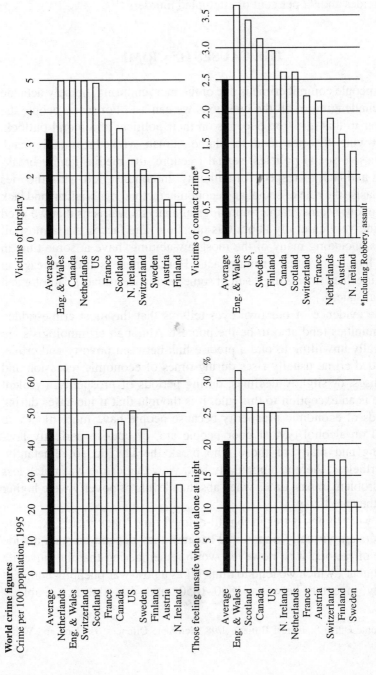

World crime figures
Crime per 100 population, 1995

Victims of burglary

Victims of contact crime*

Those feeling unsafe when out alone at night

*Including Robbery, assault

Source: International Crime Victimisation Survey, as reported in *The Guardian* 26.5.97.

Table 2: Britain's comparative crime survey

68 per cent of all violent crime was cleared up, including 91 per cent of homicides and 92 per cent of attempted murders.[11]

THE CAUSES OF CRIME

Why people commit crime is one of the most enduring, fiercely debated and challenging of all the questions we can ask. For many people the answer to this question depends on their political and moral outlook. Right-wing theories tend to blame human wickedness and greed, permissive social policies, sexual freedom, the media, family break-down and lack of respect for authority. In contrast, left-wing theories emphasise the role of social and economic factors, materialism and lack of support. Mainstream criminological analysis warns us that we need to think very carefully about this question. The fact is that almost all adults, including many of the most law-abiding, have at some time in their lives committed criminal acts. Hence, there is little mileage in thinking that crime is the result of some readily identifiable pathological mental state.

The evidence of our own eyes tells us that the most crime-ridden communities tend also to be the poorest. Although criminologists are generally unwilling to cite a precise link between poverty and crime, recorded crime usually rises during times of economic recession and stabilises, or slightly declines, during periods of prosperity. (Violent crime is an exception to this rule. It is thought that it increases during periods of economic prosperity because people have more money to spend on alcohol.) Most poor people are, of course, perfectly law-abiding and many of those who break the law do so reluctantly. Nevertheless, there is a popularly held view that crime was much less of a problem in past times when absolute levels of poverty were higher than they are today.

So were things better in that ill-defined time 'back then'? Accurate answers are virtually impossible because they depend on such a wide range of factors. It is, however, worth remembering that the 'juvenile delinquent', which we tend to think off as a post-war phenomenon, was largely invented between 1820–1850, and that the first publicly

---

[11] Home Office Statistical Bulletin 1/98, Notifiable Offences: England and Wales, 1997.

acknowledged panic about juvenile crime occurred in 1815. We know that prostitution and domestic violence were the particular pre-occupations of the Victorians — so much so that an Act preventing women and children being assaulted by their husbands and fathers had to be passed in 1853. Similarly, industrial strife was a common feature of the life of our parents, grandparents, and great-grandparents. Striking miners, for example, were shot at Featherstone in 1893, and in Tonypandy in 1911. Gunboats were even anchored in the Humber during the dock strike of 1893, and in the Mersey during the Liverpool general strike in 1911. There was a General Strike in 1926, which led to rioting in London, Glasgow and Edinburgh.

Still, levels of recorded crime were far lower in the first half of the century than they are today; yet the architects of the post-war welfare state assumed that the better social and economic conditions it created would reduce crime. In truth the causes of crime are complex, many layered and shifting. As Professor Robert Reiner, who is regarded as one of the country's leading criminologists, argues:

> . . . for a crime to occur four ingredients are necessary: motive, means, opportunity, and lack of control. There must be a motivated offender with the means to commit the crime, the opportunity presented by a vulnerable victim, and the offence must not be prevented by either external controls — police, security, etc. — or internalised controls, i.e., conscience — what the psychologist Hans Eysenck graphically called the 'inner policeman'.[12]

In this analysis the steady rise in crime between the 1950s and the 1980s, when the welfare state began to be dismantled, was due in part to the simple fact that there were many more expensive, attractive and portable goods to steal, e.g., cars, televisions, videos, hi-fis, etc. There were also important cultural changes in this period, most notably the erosion of deference and acceptance of authority. A less authoritarian culture, and the ensuing breakdown of the traditional mechanisms of social regulation, reduced the informal checks and controls that had previously prevented some people from offending. So what about the spectacular increase in crime in the 1980s? Most criminologists believe

---

[12] Robert Reiner, 'Crime and Control', LSE Magazine, Spring 1994, vol 6, No. 1, pp. 10–17.

that the crime wave was closely bound up with the adoption of free market economic policies which cut welfare benefits and increased poverty, inequality and structural unemployment, especially among the young. A significant percentage of the population was cut off from legitimate opportunities and state support at the very moment when economic success, and conspicuous consumption, seemed to be all that mattered to large swathes of British society. Researchers are agreed that the knock-on effects for certain social groups and parts of the country were devastating because of the risks of becoming the victims of crime. Not surprisingly, those excluded from the economic boom looked for alternative means of realising the new cultural goals. Whole neighbourhoods were engulfed in wave after wave of crime. Furthermore, in the search for new forms of more profitable crime, drugs came on the scene. And, as many have witnessed first hand, this did unquantifiable damage to certain neighbourhoods, increasing the levels of disorganisation, disadvantage and stigmatisation, and fuelling yet more serious forms of offending.

Anyone who doubts this link between the political and economic changes of the 1980s and the rising crime rate need look no further than France and Germany. Unlike Britain, during the 1980s both those countries maintained economic and social policies, such as a legal minimum wage and progressive taxation, which were designed to redistribute wealth and protect the poorest members of society. Both countries continued to have substantial crime and social problems, but in Germany the crime rate rose only slightly, and in France it actually fell. The fall is thought to have been due to a substantial programme of social investment, which was launched by the government of President François Mitterand in the wake of urban riots in 1981. It was recognised that unless the problems of the poor ghetto communities were addressed, there was a danger that crime would spiral out of control, and so 'social crime prevention' became accepted as the central concept of the programme. When the riots occurred, the number of recorded crimes in France was around 3.5 million, which was roughly the same as in England and Wales. By the end of the decade it had fallen to about 3 million, whereas in England and Wales it had risen to 5.5 million.[13]

---

[13] J. Pitts (1996), 'The Politics and Practice of Youth Justice', in E. McLaughlin and J. Muncie (eds), *Controlling Crime*, London: Sage, pp. 284–5.

CRIME POLICY

The rise of law and order politics

The use of law and order as a political football is a relatively recent phenomenon. An analysis of election manifestos prior to 1979 reveals that law and order was not mentioned by any party until 1959, when it was used by the Conservatives, and that Labour did not raise the issue until its election manifesto of 1966. Indeed, Labour's manifestos for the two victorious General Elections of 1974 make no comment about law and order whatsoever.[14]

The main political parties have always had quite contrasting views on law and order which reflect their wider ideological differences. Conservatism is an individualist doctrine which holds the individual to be free and rational, and therefore entirely responsible for his or her own actions. The parties of the left and centre, by contrast, believe that individual actions are shaped not only by individual will, but also by the broader social and economic context in which they occur.

The law and order card was first played to great effect by Margaret Thatcher's Conservative Party in their first successful election campaign in 1979. Thatcher eschewed the fragile post-war consensus between the main political parties — that society's ills must be tackled through social investment as well as individual actions — and instead promoted a radical new variant of the party's individualist ideology. Her approach was most famously summed up in her declaration: '... there is no such thing as society, only individuals and families'. During the 1979 campaign, on the advice of Saatchi and Saatchi, the Conservatives ran a series of adverts which linked the theme of the growth of crime with Jim Callaghan's Labour Government. One such poster is reproduced in Figure 1. The conclusion the voter was being asked to draw was an answer to the question: 'Is it safe to vote for another Labour Government?'

---

[14] D. Downes and R. Morgan, '"Hostages to Fortune"?: The Politics of Law and Order in Postwar Britain', in M. Maguire, R. Morgan and R. Reiner (eds), *The Oxford Handbook of Criminology*, Oxford: Clarendon Press, 1994, pp. 183–232.

MUGGING UP 204%
CRIMINAL DAMAGE UP 135%
ROBBERY UP 88%

Labour's record on crime is criminal. Crime is one of the few things in Britain that is booming under Labour.

In England and Wales last year, over 800,000 more crimes were recorded than in 1973. That's a rise of almost 50 per cent. And yet since Labour came to power, police strength has risen by a mere 7 per cent.

Perhaps if Labour had been more concerned with creating wealth rather than re-distributing it, they might have found it easier to be able to afford to increase policemen's pay. But it's not just more pay our policemen need. The Government have a duty to be seen to support law and order, to protect people and property.

It certainly doesn't make the police's job any easier when some Labour Ministers are seen associating themselves with potentially violent situations, as they did at Grunwick last year.

The police are doing a difficult job, in difficult times — and they need the support of all the people — and that includes Government Ministers.

Many policemen feel there's only one way they can make the Government understand their plight. And that's by leaving the force.

IS IT SAFE TO VOTE FOR ANOTHER LABOUR GOVERNMENT?
VOTE CONSERVATIVE X

Figure 1: Conservative Party publicity on crime in the 1979 General Election

The reasons why Mrs Thatcher was able to make so much of the law and order issue are many and varied. However, the events of the winter of 1978–79, dubbed 'the Winter of Discontent', are seen by many as a major turning point. Her party was able to link law-breaking and crime with mass picketing and industrial unrest and, in effect blamed the Labour Government of the day as being at the root of the problem.

Whereas the Labour Party, when it actually made comment about law and order, attempted to link crime to social factors such as unemployment, the Conservatives successfully linked it to choice, morality and personal responsibility. As we will discuss in the next chapter, it was a message that was far easier to get across to the people via the popular media than Labour's more complex analysis.

The Conservatives made good their promise to strengthen law and order by providing the police, the prison service and the other agencies within the criminal justice system with much bigger budgets, and more staff (see Table 3). They hoped that crime would fall and we would all sleep more safely in our beds, but tackling crime proved to be more difficult than the slogans on posters had led the electorate to believe. Clearly politicians had to take account of this continued rise in the crime figures, and in effect the failure of the strategy which they had introduced. If crime was still a matter of personal choice and not a consequence of social factors, why had the recorded crime figures not fallen?

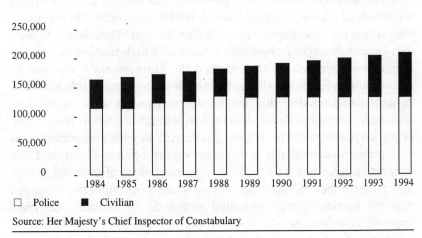

Source: Her Majesty's Chief Inspector of Constabulary

Table 3: Levels of polie and civilian staff at 31 December 1994

The Conservative election manifesto of 1987 revealed something both of the shift in emphasis on how to tackle crime, beyond giving greater resources to the police and the prison service, and of who was at fault for the continuing rise in recorded crime. The 'origins of crime', it explained:

lie deep in society in families where parents do not support or control their children; in schools where discipline is poor and in the wider world where violence is glamourised and traditional values are under attack.[15]

Views like these were indicative of the gradual re-focusing of taking 'action' on crime by preventative or control measures, such as Neighbourhood Watch and Safer Cities, and crime prevention through environmental design, including the use of closed circuit television. An independent organisation — Crime Concern — was even set up to promote this strategy, which emphasises 'active citizenship' within the community. In short, a reliance on the rule of law to tackle crime had increasingly come to be discredited and so, in the words of another government commercial, we would all have to 'crack crime together'. This in turn meant that other areas of public life would have to change, and it heralded the introduction of school 'league tables', for example, and the development of such organisations as the Child Support Agency.

By 1990 the Government was persuaded that locking up offenders, in the words of Home Secretary David Waddington, was 'an expensive way of making bad people worse'. A Government White Paper, *Crime, Justice and Protecting the Public*, much of which became law in the Criminal Justice Act 1991, signalled the Government's attempts to reserve prison for those who had committed very serious offences, and to limit the discretion that magistrates and judges were allowed in sentencing offenders. But it went further, setting out a whole philosophy of justice based on the notion of 'just deserts' in which the punishment was proportionate to the seriousness of the offence committed. Its supporters described it as the most important piece of criminal justice legislation in the UK this century. One of the most important measures was the introduction of so-called unit fines — whereby the fines imposed on offenders reflected both the seriousness of the offence, as measured in units, and the court's assessment of the offenders' disposable weekly income.

The 1991 Act ran into trouble almost immediately, and was undermined by a combination of public and political pressures. The unit

---

[15] Quoted in M. Davies, H. Croall and J. Tyrer, *Criminal Justice: An Introduction to the Criminal Justice System in England and Wales*, London and New York: Longman, 1995, p. 45.

fine system, for example, was repealed by the Criminal Justice Act 1993, which was steered through Parliament by David Waddington's successor as Home Secretary, Kenneth Clarke; and the idea of punishing less serious offenders in the community did not sit well with the increasingly punitive political climate.

Remoralisation and 'prison works'

The murder of two-year-old James Bulger by two ten-year-olds in February 1993 provoked a highly moralised debate — not just about the causes of crime, but about the very nature of British society. This crime was in many respects a defining moment in the public consciousness, because it stirred a host of fears that 1990s Britain was a menacing, violent, crime-ridden society where the most vulnerable were particularly at risk. No one listened to those who tried to calm matters by pointing out that the murder of children in Britain is extremely rare. Instead fundamental questions were posed about why the country had changed from being a bedrock of common decency marked by the rule of law, to the moral wasteland that had produced children who were incapable of understanding the difference between right and wrong. Many commentators argued that the country was in the grip of a crisis and impending social anarchy. A variety of explanations were put forward which centered on the socially disastrous consequences of the permissive social policies of the 1960s, which heralded the collapse of traditional family values; the free market economic policies of the 1980s that produced a selfish and ruthless individualism and a yobbish underclass culture; decline in religious belief; and lack of moral authority from key social institutions. One newspaper editorial after another warned politicians that they needed to take account of the depth of feeling among ordinary people about crime.

As the nation attempted to understand the Bulger murder, politicians realised that rich electoral rewards would be reaped by the party that could capture the high moral ground on crime. Both Labour and the Conservatives presented themselves as *the* party of law and order, and promised that getting a grip on crime would be the number one politicial priority. In a headline-grabbing speech, the then Shadow Home Secretary Tony Blair fired the first salvo by signalling a sea-change in Labour's policy on crime and punishment. He effectively abandoned the party's traditional emphasis on the social and economic causes of crime in favour of a new stress on moral values, and on the importance of individual responsibilities and duties. He demanded that children be taught 'the value of what is right and what is wrong'. John Major immediately responded with a highly emotive call for a new public attitude towards criminals: 'I would like the public to have a crusade against crime and change from being forgiving of crime to being considerate to the victim. Society needs to condemn a little more and understand a little less.[16]

As the moral crusades continued, the prison population gradually increased (see *Figure 2*). The new Conservative Home Secretary Michael Howard, appointed in July 1993, was clearly conscious that his Government was rapidly losing its law and order mantle to Labour. He attempted to turn the rising prison population to his advantage. In an uncompromising crime-busting speech, he told a delighted 1993 Conservative Party Conference:

> Let's make one thing absolutely clear: Prison Works. It ensures that we are protected from murderers, muggers and rapists — and it makes many who are tempted to commit crime think twice ... This may mean that more people will go to prison. I do not flinch from that. We shall no longer judge the success of our system of justice by a fall in our prison population.

The speech sounded the death knell for the progressive principles of the Criminal Justice Act 1991, and heralded one of the most dramatic shifts of thinking in the entire 18 years of Conservative rule. The 'prison works' philosophy was borrowed from the US, where its most influential advocate is the right-wing academic Charles Murray. Murray asserts that, because the risk of offenders being punished has been steadily reduced, this has resulted in a rise in crime. Likewise, the only way to stem the crime rate, he claims, is to make the risks of offending — through arrest and imprisonment — outweigh the possible advantages. In his influential but simplistic analysis, crime is in effect controlled by the threat of imprisonment. One critic has described this as a 'dimmer switch' approach to crime — 'turn the risk of imprisonment up and the crime rates fade'.[17]

---

[16] Outlined in the *Daily Mail*, 21 February 1993.

[17] Jock Young, quoted in C. Murray, with commentaries by M. Davies, A. Rutherford and J. Young, *Does Prison Work?*, Bury St Edmunds: IEA Health and Welfare Unit, 1997, p. 34.

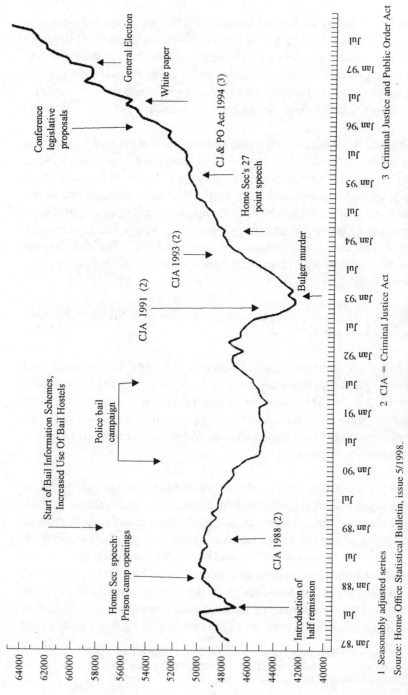

1 Seasonally adjusted series   2 CJA = Criminal Justice Act   3 Criminal Justice and Public Order Act

Source: Home Office Statistical Bulletin, issue 5/1998.

Figure 2: Prison Population and Policy Interventions 1987–1997

Iurray addressed himself to Britain's crime problem in a
cles published in the *Sunday Times*, and later published in
n the articles he was more definite than most about the date
when things started to go wrong: 'In 1955, crime began to get safer in
England'.[18] He went further, and explained with missionary zeal exactly
how this dreadful state of affairs had come about:

England of 1954 operated on the assumption that the best way to keep
crime down was to intervene early and severely. Crime was very low,
and the number of youths picked up by the police went down by about
half as children matured from their early teens to their late teens.
England today operates on the assumption that the way to deal with
crime is to be caring and forgiving of the young offender. Crime is
very high, and ... the surviving members of 1954's England, looking
at the results then and now, may be forgiven for concluding that they
were right.[19]

Michael Howard personally endorsed Murray's thesis in his own
Sunday Times article:

The risk of imprisonment in Britain did not begin to rise again until
1994. Our prison population has increased dramatically from 45,800
in 1992 to 57,000 today. My liberal critics view this increase with
horror. But, as Charles Murray showed, crime in this country has
fallen by 10 per cent ... As Charles Murray concludes, crime is low
when crime doesn't pay.

Murray's analysis specifically ignores the many tough approaches to
young people taken since 1954, such as the 'short, sharp shock' and the
use of the boot camp. However, if the relationship between the risk of
imprisonment and the crime rate was as obvious as Murray's analysis
makes it, then perhaps it really would be worth considering imprisoning
at the levels currently in existence in the United States. Yet, as we will
see in Chapter 2, the evidence does not support this thesis, even in
America. There, high rates of incarceration (over six times the British
rate) and a risk of incarceration calculated at over 11 times higher than

---

[18] C. Murray, with commentaries by M. Davies, A. Rutherford and J. Young, *Does Prison Work?*, Bury St Edmunds: IEA Health and Welfare Unit, 1997, p. 1.
[19] Murray (1997), p. 26.

in Britain have not made the United States a safer place to live in.[20] Indeed, the murder rate in the United States is seven times higher than that of Britain.

The impossibility of sustaining Murray's thesis is even more evident when we attempt to compare rates of imprisonment and crime rates within a given country, as opposed to comparing one country against another. The Netherlands, for example, doubled its rate of imprisonment between 1987 and 1995, during which time the increase in the crime rate was 8 per cent. During the same period in Scotland there was a 4 per cent increase in imprisonment and only a 4 per cent increase in the crime rate, half the rate that there was in The Netherlands.[21] These examples are merely the tip of the iceberg, refuting the hypothesis that Murray and others have been peddling. What is clear is that the risk of imprisonment is merely one of many factors which determines the crime rate, and that it is by no means the dominant factor. After all, how people perceive the risk of imprisonment will differ from person to person depending on their age, circumstances, colour, and class. Thus the crime rate seems to be determined more by patterns of employment, the use of illegal drugs, and levels of informal control within the community, than by the risk of imprisonment.

In 1994, Michael Howard suggested that a 5.5 per cent fall in recorded crime, the largest single drop in 40 years, was a vindication of his 'prison works' policies and evidence that the Government was winning the war on crime. These claims need to be treated with the utmost caution, because, as we have seen, recorded crime figures often fall during periods of relative economic prosperity. Violent crime actually increased in 1994, which was ironic given that Howard had declared that his policies would help protect the public from murderers, muggers and rapists. The overall fall in the recorded crime figures was later attributed to 'cuffing' — the dishonest practice of the police not recording crimes which had been reported — or more simply to the police 'cooking the books'.[22] Moreover, Howard ignored the fact that, if the BCS is to be believed, the actual, as opposed to the recorded, levels of crime may have actually increased. As we shall see in Chapter 2, 25 years of 'prison works' policies in the US have done nothing to alleviate that country's crime problem.

---

[20] *ibid.*, p. 34.

[21] *ibid.*, p. 34.

[22] See the report in *The Sunday Times*, 16 October 1994.

Despite the poverty of the 'prison works' arguments, the Labour Opposition, in its desperation to sidestep Conservative accusations that it was 'soft on crime', did not vote against Howard's highly controversial Criminal Justice and Public Order Act 1994.

The remoralisation of the crime debate intensified in the aftermath of the Dunblane Massacre, the Frederick and Rosemary West case, and the murder of head teacher Philip Lawrence. And in the run-up to the 1997 election both political parties vied with each other to come up with populist soundbites to prove who was the toughest on crime. Tony Blair's successor as Shadow Home Secretary, Jack Straw, claimed that the Conservatives were soft on crime, and promised action to re-claim the streets from beggars, squeegee merchants, noisy neighbours, vandals, under-age drinkers and threatening children. In a desperate attempt to re-seize the initiative on law and order, Michael Howard promised voters that a re-elected Conservative Government would intensify its moral crusade against crime by implementing minimum jail sentences, toughen up community punishments, build more private prisons, extend closed circuit television, introduce identity cards and support 'zero tolerance' policing.

The Conservatives' last major piece of legislation, the Crime (Sentences) Act, was passed just before the 1997 general election. It introduced mandatory minimum sentences for certain categories of repeat offenders and abolished automatic remission. Many believed it to be a triumph of crude political expediency over common sense. Indeed, when the Act's provisions were being discussed in the House of Lords, no less a figure than the former Lord Chief Justice of England, Lord Taylor, commented: 'Never in the history of our criminal law have such far-reaching proposals been put forward on the strength of such flimsy evidence.' Despite such criticisms, the Labour party, in a bid to neutralise law and order at the forthcoming election, helped vote the Act through Parliament.

Whither New Labour?

At the end of all of this, where has the New Labour Government left to go? Despite supporting the Act, during the last months of opposition Jack Straw continued to distance his party from some aspects of Conservative policy. He called prison privatisation 'morally repugnant' and, perhaps more significantly, appeared to reject the 'prison works' philosophy, stating: 'I do not believe that the public feel reassured by the rising prison population.'[23]

Tony Blair's famous soundbite, 'tough on crime and tough on the causes of crime', allowed Labour to be seen as taking a Conservative-style hard line on law and order, while maintaining the traditional socialist insistence that social factors play a role in crime.

Jack Straw's flagship Crime and Disorder Bill reflects the schizo-phrenia of the 'tough on crime, tough on the causes of crime' stance. As we will see in Chapter 4, most of its measures are aimed at young offenders. Straw has attempted to fend off his liberal critics by emphasising that some of the most important measures are designed to divert young offenders away from the courts. He has also won cautious praise from prison reformers for measures such as compulsory treatment for drug addicts and the early release, under electronic tag-enforced curfews, of up to 6,000 prisoners a year.

The Bill was heralded as a clear departure from Michael Howard's policies, yet during its first year in power the New Labour Government's practical difficulties in distancing itself from those policies have become all too apparent. Jack Straw has approved more prison privatisation than all of his Conservative predecessors combined, and, as we will see in the next chapter, the prison population has reached its highest ever levels under New Labour. 'Prison works', it seems, is alive and well, and it is 'business as usual' at the Home Office.

---

[23] J. Straw, 'The Penal System in Crisis', in D. Bean (ed.), *Law Reform for All*, London: Blackstone Press, 1996, p. 31.

2　Prisons

Christopher Morgan is a retired business executive turned farmer who, through the Prison Reform Trust's penfriends scheme, began an exchange of letters with the life-sentenced prisoner, Tom Shannon. As their correspondence grew, and their friendship and trust in each other developed, Shannon allowed his new penfriend a glimpse into prison life. Here was a world of drug trafficking and addiction; of stabbings and male rape; of misery and the general futility of it all. Morgan, who runs furniture-restoring weekends at his farm, was unaccustomed to what was being described. He wrote: 'Everything you say is new and a revelation to me ... what terrifying places gaols are ... you don't realise that what seems ordinary to you is absolutely extraordinary to an innocent like me.'[1]

Few people have been prepared to expose themselves to the realities of prison life in the way that Morgan has, and as a consequence there is very little understanding about what happens 'inside'. This chapter assesses the current state of the prison system in England and Wales, with regard to the rising prison population, the expenditure on prisons and their implications. The influence of politics on the prison population will also be discussed, as will the reconviction rates of ex-prisoners. The figures would suggest that prison is 'an expensive way of making bad people worse'. However, the picture is not completely pessimistic, and several examples of good practice in prisons will be outlined.

---

[1] T. Shannon and C. Morgan, *Invisible Crying Tree*, London: Black Swan Books, 1997, p. 17 and p. 105.

THE PRISON POPULATION

Since 1993, Britain has been in the midst of an unprecedented prison boom. The number of inmates held in our prisons has risen from around 49,000 in 1987 to 63,868 in November 1997, the highest ever level. The prison population is predicted to reach 82,800 during 2005, provided that current trends continue. So intense was the pressure on HM Prison Service to cope with these numbers that it was forced to bring into operation *HMP The Weare*, a ship that had been converted into a floating prison.

In 1996 the UK imprisoned 110 people per 100,000, which made it second only to Portugal (140 per 100,000) as one of the most punitive countries in Western Europe (see Table 4). As we discussed in Chapter 1, the boom was partly the result of the US-style 'prison works' philosophy and policies of the last Conservative Home Secretary Michael Howard. Changes in the early release scheme under the Criminal Justice Act 1991 also resulted in some inmates staying in prison for longer periods.

England and Wales	110
Northern Ireland	100
Scotland	110
Belgium	80
France	90
Germany	90
Italy	90
Spain	110
Portugal	140

Table 4: Prison population per 100,000 of general population 1996

Young people and those from unskilled backgrounds make up the bulk of our prison populations. Afro-Caribbeans make up 1 per cent of the national population: they account for 11 per cent of the prison population (see Table 5).

England and Wales — 30 June 1997

Number of persons and *percentages*

Sex of prisoner	Total		White		Black²		South Asian³		Chinese & Other⁴		Unrecorded	
	number	*per cent*	number	*per cent*	number	*per cent*	number	*per cent*	number	*per cent*	number	*per cent*
Males and females												
1992	45,486	*100*	37,705	*83*	4,773	*10*	1,388	*3*	1,043	*2*	577	*1*
1993	44,246	*100*	36,855	*83*	5,013	*11*	1,356	*3*	926	*2*	96	*–*
1994	48,879	*100*	40,754	*83*	5,606	*11*	1,347	*3*	1,102	*2*	70	*–*
1995	51,084	*100*	42,207	*83*	5,982	*12*	1,497	*3*	1,318	*3*	80	*–*
1996	55,256	*100*	45,029	*81*	6,986	*13*	1,654	*3*	1,524	*3*	63	*–*
1997	61,467	*100*	50,000	*81*	7,658	*12*	1,920	*3*	1,887	*3*	2	*–*
Males												
1992	43,950	*100*	36,616	*83*	4,464	*10*	1,363	*3*	981	*2*	526	*1*
1993	42,666	*100*	33,691	*84*	4,690	*11*	1,335	*3*	854	*2*	96	*–*
1994	47,075	*100*	39,399	*84*	4,236	*11*	1,320	*3*	1,050	*2*	70	*–*
1995	49,086	*100*	40,697	*83*	4,592	*11*	1,470	*3*	1,247	*3*	80	*–*
1996	52,951	*100*	43,280	*82*	6,538	*12*	1,629	*3*	1,441	*3*	63	*–*
1997	58,795	*100*	47,966	*82*	7,152	*12*	1,895	*3*	1,780	*3*	2	*–*
Females												
1992	1,536	*100*	1,089	*71*	309	*20*	25	*2*	62	*4*	51	*3*
1993	1,580	*100*	1,164	*74*	323	*20*	21	*1*	72	*5*	–	*–*
1994	1,804	*100*	1,355	*75*	370	*21*	27	*1*	52	*3*	–	*–*
1995	1,998	*100*	1,510	*76*	390	*20*	27	*1*	71	*4*	–	*–*
1996	2,305	*100*	1,749	*76*	448	*19*	26	*1*	83	*4*	–	*–*
1997	2,672	*100*	2,034	*76*	506	*19*	25	*1*	107	*4*	–	*–*

Ethnic origin(1)

(1) Prior to 1993 coding of ethnic origin was similar to that used in the EC Labour Force Survey. In 1993 a new ethnic classification system was adopted in prisons which is congruent with that used for the Census of Population. The change in coding means that figures for 1992 and 1993–97 are not directly comparable.

(2) In 1992 ethnic origin classification was 'West Indian, Guyanese, African'

(3) In 1992 ethnic origin classification was 'Indian, Pakistani, Bangladeshi'

(4) In 1992 ethnic origin classification was 'Chinese, Arab, Mixed Origin'

Source: Home Office Statistical Bulletin, Issue 5/1998

Table 5: Population in Prison by sex and ethnic group(1)

New Labour — new records

There is no guarantee that much will change under the new Labour administration. One of the reasons for Labour's May 1997 landslide election victory was that they had begun to talk tough on crime, and in their desperation to be elected they considered it too risky to criticise the 'prison works' philosophy. A few weeks prior to the election the future Home Secretary Jack Straw admitted on the *Newsnight* programme that the prison population was likely to rise further before it falls. His prophecy is borne out by Home Office statistics which show that the prison population rose by almost 3 per cent during the first six months of the new Labour Government. Despite stating that he found privatisation 'repugnant', Jack Straw has nonetheless sanctioned its extension within the prison service.

Through such measures as the extended use of electronic tagging and the early release of prisoners, Labour's Crime and Disorder Bill was supposed to cut the prison population by around 10 per cent, but the Home Office's own figures suggest that this is a mere pipe dream. The problem is partially the legacy of Michael Howard's Crime (Sentences) Act, which was passed with Labour support just before the 1997 General Election. In April 1997 the Home Office estimated that it would increase the prison population by at least 10,700 over the next 15 years. In January 1998 the estimate was revised dramatically upwards to as much as 30,000 — almost 50 per cent of the 1997 total — in just seven years.[2] The Director General of the Prison Service, Richard Tilt, acknowledged that the situation had changed 'quite radically' since the April 1997 estimate.[3]

Who is caught up in the prison boom?

As we will argue in the next chapter, the prison boom has been fuelled by public fears about violent crime which do not accord with reality. In his original 'prison works' speech, Conservative Home Secretary Michael Howard directly addressed these fears, telling his audience that incarceration 'ensures that we are protected from murderers, muggers and rapists'. Few would argue with the proposition that serious violent

---

[2] Home Office Statistical Bulletin, *Revised Projections of Long Term Trends in the Prison Population to 2005*, by Philip White and Iqbal Powar, 29 January 1998.

[3] 'Prison numbers to rise by 50pc' *The Guardian*, 29 January 1998.

criminals should be locked up, but the fact is that the vast majority of prisoners are not convicted of murder, mugging or rape, or indeed of lesser crimes of violence. Of the 60,000 people sentenced to immediate custody in 1995, 76 per cent were convicted of non-violent offences. The following figures give a more complete breakdown:

- violence against the person — 8,300
- sexual offences — 2,400
- burglary — 13,400
- robbery — 3,300
- theft and handling — 15,600
- fraud and forgery — 3,300
- criminal damage — 1,000
- drug offences — 5,300
- other (excluding motoring) — 5,800
- motoring — 1,600.

What of the 20,000 extra prisoners convicted between 1993 and 1997 — were they murderers, muggers and rapists? Well no, in fact the vast majority were non-violent offenders. For instance, between 1994 and 1995, 6,900 (13 per cent) more people were sentenced to immediate custody than in the previous year.[4] The most rapid rise was for non-violent offenders. For example, 20 per cent more people were sent to prison for theft and handling stolen goods, but there was only a 1 per cent rise in those sent to prison for violence against the person. More recent figures show a different story. Between 1991 and 1996, there was, overall, a 6 per cent rise in the number of offenders sentenced to prison for theft and handling stolen goods. The corresponding figure for those convicted of violence against the person saw a 14 per cent rise. Despite this, of the 84,600 people who received prison sentences in 1996, 20,157 were convicted for non-payment of fines.

In 1996, a total of 61,000 people were remanded in custody, which was approximately 12 per cent of those remanded overall. The average time on remand was 56 days for men and 43 for women, but many people are remanded for considerably longer periods. In the eyes of the law these people are innocent until proven guilty, yet they frequently

---

[4] All figures calculated from *Criminal Statistics England and Wales*, Cmnd 3764, London: HMSO, 1996.

have to endure the worst conditions in over-crowded local prisons. Of course many are there for good reasons, such as their previous criminal record, or the seriousness of the crime of which they are accused, but 66 per cent of remanded men and 53 per cent of remanded women were subsequently acquitted or given a non-custodial sentence. One could conclude, therefore, that there are many offenders in prison who do not represent any physical danger to the public and whose offences are very minor in legal terms. Is it necessary to imprison such offenders?

An expensive way...

The total running costs for HM Prison Service for the financial year 1994 were £1,510m. In 1996 it cost from £269 a week (or £14,000 pa) to keep an adult male in an open prison; and in a high security dispersal prison that figure rises to £659 per week (or £34,000 pa). This compares to fees of £8,000 pa at the average British public school, and approximately £6,000 pa for an overseas student studying in a British university.

Each new prison costs an average of £90m. The prison population is currently rising by 300 per week, which means that a new prison needs to open approximately every fortnight. Twenty new prisons have been built since 1985, but, as we have seen, the demand for new places is outstripping supply at a frightening rate. At the present rate of growth, it has been calculated by the Home Office (January 1998) that £2b would be required to build up to 24 new prisons. In February 1998, Home Secretary Jack Straw quietly announced that an emergency £70m payment would be made to help the prison service cope with the increased numbers. It came just a few months after a similar payment of £47m. The combined total was more than five times the amount that the Government committed to the first stage of its flagship programme to reduce primary school class sizes.

... of making bad people worse

Prison might keep dangerous people off the street, but on the whole it does not make them better people — anything but. The prison service monitors the future criminal convictions of all inmates who are released from prison, and the statistics make depressing reading. The most recent data date back to 1992. Within two years 51 per cent of the total had been reconvicted, and for young men under the age of 18 the figure was 72 per cent. A four-year study of prisoners released in 1987 was even more depressing, with an average of 67 per cent reconvicted and as many as 92 per cent of young men aged 15 to 16 re-offending (see Table 6).

Within two years (from 1992)		*Within four years (from 1987)*	
Adult males	45%	Adult males	60%
Adult females	38%	All young males	82%
Young males	72%	Males 15 to 16	92%
Young females	51%	All males	68%
Average	51%	Adult women	44%
		All young females	61%
		Females 15 to 16	55%
		All females	48%
		Average	67%

Table 6: Percentage of people released from custody who were reconvicted

One might expect that the people who had originally been given longer sentences would be the more hardened criminals and therefore most likely to be reconvicted. But in fact the highest reconviction rate within two years (57 per cent) was for those who had served less than 12 months. It fell to 47 per cent for those who had served between 12 months and 4 years, and to 26 per cent for those who had served between 4 and 10 years.

Property offenders tended to be reconvicted far more than violent offenders. For example, 33 per cent of those released from sentence for theft and handling stolen goods, compared to only 8 per cent of those released from sentence for violence against the person.

Perhaps the most depressing aspect of these statistics is that they record only the number of former prisoners who are reconvicted. The numbers who return to crime are likely to be higher because many don't get caught.

Why do so many former prisoners return to crime? Most people who know about prisons — whether they be prison, probation, or police officers, or the prisoners themselves — testify that prisons tend to breed crime. There are four basic reasons:

- *Prisons are academies of crime* Prisons tend to house the masters of almost every kind of criminal act. Unless the prison can provide a constructive regime which can usefully occupy the time of first-time prisoners and help them to address their offending behaviour, it is inevitable that they will learn new skills from the more experienced inmates. The reconviction rates recorded above would seem to support this view.

- *Prison affects the way people view themselves* Crime is generally an anti-social activity, and tends to be committed by people who feel that they have no stake in society and therefore few responsibilities towards it. Prison removes them even further from society and, all too often, reinforces their anti-social inclinations.

- *Ex-prisoners can't get work* Even those people who emerge from prison as reformed characters, determined to go straight, find it extremely difficult to find work and that most of the jobs that are available are casual and poorly paid. In such circumstances many risk returning to their more lucrative criminal pursuits. In 1997, a NACRO survey of ex-offenders looking for work found that many of these ex-offenders lived in areas of high unemployment. Most of those who did find work, found only part-time, temporary or casual low-paid jobs. In addition to the handicap of a criminal record, many of them are hindered by a lack of skills and qualifications.

- *The family effect* Because prison often deprives families of their main breadwinners, remaining family members may sometimes turn to crime to make ends meet. The effect on the children of prisoners is more insidious, as they can often grow up viewing incarceration as a normal part of adult life. This, of course, does not mean that they are doomed to a life of crime, but mothers and fathers of children whose other parent is in prison inevitably face a tough challenge in trying to bring up a family single-handed. For female prisoners who have young babies, four of the women's prisons have mother and baby units; but even then they provide a total of only 64 places, caring for babies up to 18 months old. Chapter 6 ('Women in the Criminal Justice System') discusses this issue further.

As we will see in Chapters 8 and 9, there are far cheaper and more effective alternatives to prison which don't carry the same social costs.

LESSONS FROM AMERICA

Since the current prison boom was based on ideas borrowed directly from America, it is to America that we should look to gauge their likely effects in this country.

Whereas Britain's prison population has been rising for less than five years, in America it has been rising for 25 years. The most dramatic rise, of over 300 per cent, has taken place over the last 15 years, with the total number of people incarcerated in federal and state prisons and local jails now standing at over 1.6 million (see Table 7). In some states the rate of increase has been even more dramatic. For example, in California it has increased sixfold since the late 1970s, and Texas, New Hampshire and Colorado even outstripped that.[5]

Year	State and federal prisons	Jails	Total	% change
1980	329,821	163,994	493,815	
				212.7%
1994	1,053,738	490,442	1,544,180	

Table 7: Prison population in the USA, 1980 and 1994

Source: S. R. Donziger, *The Real War on Crime*, New York: Harper Collins, 1996

In 1996, America's rate of incarceration was 555 per 100,000 people, around four times higher than any other Western country and second only to Russia (710 per 100,000) among the world's democratic nations.

America's prison population accounts for 2 per cent of the male labour force; and if they were included in the country's unemployment statistics, the male jobless rate would rise by about a third to 8 per cent. The disproportionate number of black prisoners means that the effect on

---

[5] Donziger, Steve (ed), *The Real War on Crime*, New York: Harper Collins, 1996.

the black male employment rate would be even more pronounced, rising from 11 per cent to 19 per cent.

In addition to the 1.6 million prisoners, 3.6 million people are on probation or parole. Thus overall there are 5 million people being supervised within the criminal justice system, which accounts for 3 per cent of the US adult population.

As in Britain, the majority of the prisoners have not committed a violent offence. Of the 1.6 million who are in prison at any one time, 65 per cent were non-violent offenders. But if the number who are annually admitted to prison is considered, the percentage of non-violent offenders is even higher: 73 per cent in state prisons and 94 per cent in federal prisons. The boom in prison numbers has, likewise, been fuelled by non-violent offenders. Of the million extra people in prison in 1994 compared to 1980, only 16 per cent had been convicted of crimes of violence.

The costs of the prison boom, both financial and social, have been vast. Between 1980 and 1993, for example, federal spending on correctional facilities increased by 521 per cent, but over the same period, federal spending on employment and training programmes was cut almost in half.

Similar changes have taken place at a state level. California alone is spending over $3.6b on prisons in the current financial year. This represents a threefold rise in just 10 years and has led to savage cuts in education and social services. Louisiana is one of the poorest states in the union, yet it was able to find money for a prison expansion programme which gave it the third highest rate of incarceration in the country. At the same time a report by the US General Accounting Office described the schools in the state's largest city, New Orleans, as 'rotting away' through 'hundreds of millions of dollars worth of uncorrected water and termite damage'. The report highlighted similar problems in other states.

Critics of America's prison boom believe that such changes in the pattern of public spending have effected a fundamental shift in the relationship between America's poor and their public institutions. According to Professor Elliott Currie of the University of California, prison has become: 'Something it [has] never been in our history — in some respects the chief agency for dealing with the social problems of the most disadvantaged people in America.'[6]

---

[6] E. Currie, *Is America Really Winning the War on Crime?*, London: NACRO (1996).

For all these worrying facts and figures, even the critics of the prison boom expected that the so-called 'incapacitation effect' would result in reduced crime levels. Their best estimates were for a reduction of around 20 per cent in violent crime, but this has proved to be overly optimistic.

True, there have been some recent dramatic falls in crime. For example, since 1991 the homicide rate has dropped by about 16 per cent nationally and reported robbery has dropped by around 20 per cent. It should be remembered, however, that in the seven years prior to 1991, when prison numbers were also spiralling upwards, recorded violent crime rose sharply: murder by 24 per cent and robbery by 33 per cent. More importantly, these figures reflect only those crimes that are reported to the police. The National Crime Victimisation Survey, which, like the BCS, is based on data from victims of crime rather than from police forces, suggested that there was no decline in serious violent crime between 1992 and 1994.

If the whole 25-year period is considered, the impact of America's prison expansion on violent crime is at best patchy and at worst dismal. There have been welcome falls in the homicide rate of some cities such as Boston (3 per cent) and San Francisco (13 per cent), but nationally the rate has, if anything, crept slightly upwards. Some cities have witnessed sharp rises: in Detroit, for example, it rose by 41 per cent; in Los Angeles by 71 per cent; in Memphis by 95 per cent; in Milwaukee by 213 per cent; in Minneapolis by 305 per cent; and in New Orleans by 329 per cent. Some states have seen even sharper rises, for example 417 per cent in New York and 467 per cent in Arizona.

Unfortunately the US public and politicians alike have short memories, and prefer to stick with the notion that the 'get tough' policies have worked. New York City is often cited as evidence of the success of the tough line on crime, but a close analysis casts doubt on this claim. The more recent sharp falls in the city's crime figures come off the back of dramatic increases in the late 1980s, which were largely due to a crack epidemic that has since waned considerably. That epidemic and the murders that went with it, together with other factors such as AIDS, pushed the death rate for young men, especially African-Americans, sky-high in the low income neighbourhoods of New York and other large cities. Since it was this section of the population that was at far the most at risk from violent crime, the reduction in their numbers may, in itself, have contributed to the falling crime rate.

Faced with unconvincing statistics on the effect of the prison boom on crime levels, the prisons lobby argues that, without the increase in incarceration, crime rates would be even higher. It is an argument that is impossible to disprove. However, studies show that some of the less punitive states, such as Massachusetts, have seen declines in violent crime, whereas some of the most punitive, such as Virginia and Arizona, have seen some of the sharpest rises. More importantly the 'prison works' argument assumes that the alternative to locking people up is to do nothing, whereas the reality is that convicted offenders would be given non-custodial sentences.

Despite the huge costs of mass incarceration, the prisons lobby has attempted to argue that it is cost-effective to lock people up. The cost of building prisons, they claim, is offset by the savings made through preventing crime. A notorious study by the Governor of California's office calculated that 'Three strikes and you're out' would prevent 7,000 murders a year, even though the state has never suffered more than 4,000 murders a year.

A Department of Justice study estimated the total cost of crime to be $450b a year. This suggests that the $40b pa spent on incarceration was relatively low — a bizarre leap of logic, not least because the $450b is a complete fiction. The figure was arrived at by building in enormous costs for the pain and suffering of the victims. Clearly the impact of crimes is very important, but it is impossible and disingenuous to put a price on them. Without those costs the figure dropped to $105b, which, according to the Department of Justice, still represented a saving of $65b. But this money did not exist in reality — it was merely a projection, and an unprovable one at that.

An earlier Department of Justice study made even more outrageous claims, namely that the imprisonment of one inmate saves the country $430,000 a year. The figure was reached by making the extraordinary assumption that each prisoner would commit 187 street crimes a year, at the cost to the victims of $2,300 per crime.

WHAT KIND OF PRISON SYSTEM SHOULD WE HAVE?

The mood and temper of the public in regard to the treatment of crime and criminals is one of the most unfailing tests of the civilisation of any country.

These words were not uttered by a soft liberal reformer, but by the former Conservative Prime Minister Winston Churchill in 1910. His words are as relevant today as they were at the beginning of the century. Indeed, having served time as a prisoner of war during the Boer War, Churchill was one of the very few political leaders to have experienced the misery of incarceration first hand.

Although it is our belief that the British prison population is currently too high, some criminals clearly need to be locked up, both as a punishment to them and to protect society. The question is, what type of prison system should we be locking them up in? The general answer has to be one that makes them better people when they come out. HM Prison Service's mission statement, issued in 1988, pays lip service to this idea: 'Her Majesty's Prison Service serves the public by keeping in custody those committed by the courts. Our duty is to look after them with humanity and help them lead law-abiding and useful lives in custody and after release.'

To read some tabloid newspaper accounts, many of Britain's prisons are holiday camps in which prisoners lounge around watching TV, work out in luxury gymnasia and order take-away curries. In fact, the vast majority of prisoners will testify that being locked up away from their friends and families is in itself a deeply traumatic experience. Added to that, the physical and psychological conditions in many jails leave a lot to be desired, and in some cases are appalling. Hardly a month goes by without a report by Her Majesty's Chief Inspector of Prisons, General Sir David Ramsbotham (an ex-military man who was not chosen for his soft liberal views), highlighting such conditions. In March 1997, for example, his report on Dover Young Offenders Institution described it as a 'jungle' in which the inmates had to 'fight to survive, or exist as a vulnerable prisoner subjected to continual intimidation and insult'. Many of the worst aspects of prison life are known only to the prisoners and their officers. Such conditions only serve to make prisoners worse. To become better people they need, first and foremost, their dignity.

The massive riot in 1990 at Strangeways Prison in Manchester, was a dramatic confirmation of the dangers of denying prisoners their dignity. A prison designed to accommodate 970 prisoners was holding 1,647, at least two to a cell. The lack of in-cell sanitation meant that the majority of prisoners were forced to go through the early morning ritual of slopping-out. This combination had a cumulative effect on the regime provision: visits were infrequent and brief, and the educational programmes were oversubscribed. In addition there were few out-of-cell activities and little opportunity for physical exercise. Treated like animals, the prisoners eventually reacted like animals, with devastating consequences.

Lord Justice Woolf's inquiry into the riot looked far beyond the immediate problems of Strangeways and considered the deeper malaise within the prison system. His report concluded that the poor physical conditions were part of a much broader problem of the manner in which inmates were treated. Although they did not necessarily express it in such terms, most of the prisoners he spoke to 'felt a lack of justice'.

If prisoners were to have a reasonable chance of being reformed by the system, and if future trouble was to be avoided, this fundamental issue would have to be addressed. Woolf therefore opposed the received wisdom that prisoners' goods and services should be regarded as privileges to be awarded or removed by discretion. He referred instead to prisoners' 'threshold quality of life' and to their 'legitimate expectations' about their treatment. They would also need practical measures such as education, drink and drug therapy, and counselling. Indeed there has been recent primary research into the role of education in effecting personal change in prisoners, not only through the acquisition of practical skills and knowledge, but also through fostering self-esteem and skills in communication.[7]

Woolf's ideas were not new, but it was the first time that they had been articulated by such an influential source. More importantly, the report focused on the inmates' sense of injustice at terrible prison conditions. Not all of his report's recommendations were formally adopted, but they were generally warmly welcomed by most interested parties, including prisoners, and the report was viewed as a blueprint for the future. Unfortunately, within five years the cause of prison reform had suffered a series of major blows.

In 1993, the hardliner Michael Howard became Home Secretary. In his determination to 'out-tough' the Labour Party on crime, the cause of prison reform was fair game. 'If you can't do the time, don't do the crime' he told his party's 1993 annual conference during his 'prison works' speech, clearly indicating that he had no problem with the idea that prisons should seek to punish rather than reform.

---

[7] A. Reuss, *Higher Education and Personal Change in Prisoners*, research paper presented to the Dispersals Conference, December 1997. All references to the Woolf enquiry taken from 'Prison Disturbances, April 1990 (*Woolf Report*) (1991) CM 1456 London: HMSO.

Howard gained momentum from a rash of new stories suggesting that prisoners had an easy life; but ironically the events that most set back the Woolf agenda — the breakouts from the top security Whitemoor and Parkhurst prisons, in September 1994 and January 1995 respectively — almost cost him his job. Prison security suddenly shot to the top of the political agenda, and in the face of mounting parliamentary pressure Howard ordered inquiries into both escapes, and eventually sacked the Prison Service's Director General Derek Lewis. The Whitemoor inquiry, carried out by Sir John Woodcock with the assistance of 11 police officers, and the Parkhurst inquiry, carried out by General Sir John Learmont, focused narrowly on security. They were used by Howard to shift the emphasis of penal policy away from the concepts of justice and rehabilitation that had been pursued in the Woolf report, and towards the containment and control of prisoners. As a result of Learmont's recommendations security became ever tighter, and not just in high security prisons but throughout the prison system. Closed visits were introduced, with no contact between exceptional high-risk inmates and their visitors. Visitors were searched more thoroughly going into prisons, and staff also began to be searched going in to and out of work. Dedicated search teams were introduced, the use of closed circuit television was expanded, and there was a major drugs crackdown.

Mandatory drug testing (MDT) was introduced into prisons in 1995, as part of the Government's aim of reducing the level of drug misuse in prisons. It led to two major problems: first, prisoners tested as positive were not always linked into any planned drug treatment programme; secondly, MDT seemed to be encouraging users to switch to hard drugs, which are less easily detected than soft drugs. In the words of one recent research study, MDT is 'primarily an indiscriminate punitive regime that is adding to the overcrowding in British prisons by effectively adding extra weeks to prisoners' sentences'. The study also observed that the MDT has not been matched by a planned development in drug rehabilitation programmes.[8]

Michael Howard's realignment of the prison service took place during a period when it had to face two further daunting factors. The first was an over-crowding crisis prompted by the 50 per cent increase in prison numbers in just over five years. Each week the service had to

---

[8] M. MacDonald, 'Mandatory Drug Testing', *Prison Service Journal*, January 1998, No. 115.

find 300 new spaces in a system that was already full to bursting. The second problem was a 12 per cent cut in its budget for 1996/97 announced by Howard, which created unbearable pressure on already limited resources.

As a consequence of these factors, prisoners have found themselves being shunted around the prison system, often long distances from their families. To stay within budgets governors have had to cut work, physical education, and drink and drug rehabilitation programmes. Three hundred prison teachers have been sacked, and some prisons have lost 80 per cent of their education programmes. At the same time many prisoners are locked away for longer with nothing to do. Many people with experience of the prison system believe it is once again becoming a powder keg set to explode.

GOOD PRISONS IN ACTION

For all the difficulties that it faces, much good work is done within the prison system which can be built upon. The following three examples show what can be achieved if prisoners and staff work together, and feel they have a stake in each others' success.[9]

Lancaster Farms Young Offenders Institution

The prison was designed as a category C adult male training prison to take over the role of nearby Lancaster prison. By the time governor David Waplington was appointed in February 1992, population pressures in the North West of England forced the prison service to keep Lancaster prison open and to turn Lancaster Farms into a young offenders institution, two-thirds of which would house unsentenced remand prisoners and the remaining third sentenced prisoners. An already difficult situation was compounded when its population expanded to 378, without any extra staff, and the more volatile remand population rose to well beyond two-thirds of the total.

Despite the potential for major control problems, Lancaster Farms fared well. Following his inspection in November 1994, the then HM Chief Inspector of Prisons Judge Stephen Tumim commented:

---

[9] The accounts of these prisons are taken from D. Wilson and S. Bryans, 'The Prison Governor: Theory and Practice', *Leyhill: Prison Service Journal* (1998) pp. 142–156.

There were many indications of a well-run, safe and constructive establishment ... cells were the tidiest and cleanest we have seen; evening association was more like a first class, well-organised boys' club than a remand centre. Every adolescent had an opportunity to attend education, training or work which was relevant.

The Chief Inspector's report set out the reasons for the success:

We found strong leadership from the governor and his senior management team and this, in turn, gave staff confidence in their own abilities and allowed them to develop initiatives. The establishment's Statement of Purpose — 'Our aim is to prevent the next victim' — was typical of the positive message going out to both staff and inmates.

The 'strong leadership' was based on the governor doing the following:

- working long hours and maintaining high levels of visibility round the prison
- communicating directly and openly with both staff and inmates
- making staff feel confident about putting forward ideas, creating initiatives and managing inmates. Each day he or his deputy would meet with representatives from all areas at a team briefing, which was then relayed to individual teams the following day. He would also routinely attend meetings chaired by his managers
- involving everyone in a multi-disciplinary approach and encouraging cooperation between departments
- openly rewarding good work and giving only constructive criticism
- talking to all new members of staff during their week-long induction, in order to set out the prison's ethos
- working with the Trust for Adolescence to create specific training packs for staff who work with young inmates and female inmates. Several young offenders institutions, such as Brinsford, Glen Parva and Huntercombe, have adopted this training pack
- setting clear standards of behaviour for inmates, which involved the creation of a comprehensive anti-bullying strategy
- creating a system of rewards and sanctions which gave a clear structure to inmates with histories of non-conforming behaviour.

Brixton

In the early 1990s, Brixton was a prison with huge problems. It regularly held upwards of 1,100 prisoners, over 50 per cent more than it was designed to, with the majority still slopping-out. There were 14 suicides between 1989 and 1990, many in the notorious 'F' wing which housed mentally ill prisoners. The 1990 report by HM Chief Inspector of Prisons Judge Stephen Tumim described it as 'a corrupting and depressing institution', and the following year it was among those British prisons to be condemned by the European Committee for the Prevention of Torture.

Following the armed breakout by IRA prisoners Nessan Quinlevan and Pearse McCauley in July 1991, a new governor from the Scottish prison service, Dr Andrew Coyle, was appointed with a brief to improve the prison's disastrous record. One of his priorities was to close 'F' wing, which was achieved by transferring the disturbed prisoners to one of five health-care wards where they received better medical attention. Potentially suicidal prisoners were no longer held in cells, but were held in small wards where they could mix with other prisoners and where staff had time to listen to them. The Press was allowed to view the prison, and external organisations such as the Department of Health, NACRO and the Prison Reform Trust were encouraged to send representatives into the prison on a regular basis to help prisoners prepare for release.

Aware that long-term success could be achieved only through staff and management working together towards recognised goals, Coyle instigated a strategic planning exercise called 'Brixton 2000'. A senior management team drew up a broad plan. Staff were encouraged to study this, to consider how it affected their area of work, and to offer suggestions as to how it might be improved. Following this period of consultation a plan emerged to which everyone had contributed and in which they felt they had a stake. Its aims included the transformation of Brixton into a community prison; the development of a team approach to problems; and improving the relationship between staff and prisoners. The plan was underpinned by a shared set of values, based on openness, fairness and justice, to which all staff were asked to subscribe, in return for a high commitment from the management to the staff.

Coyle's initiatives have paid dividends. When he inspected the prison in 1996, Judge Tumim's successor, Sir David Ramsbotham, commented that it had 'improved significantly in the last three years and is now a well managed, well ordered and more caring establishment'.

Grendon Underwood

The prison at Grendon Underwood opened in 1963 and remains the only prison in England and Wales — and one of the few in the world — which operates as a therapeutic community. Its first governor, the psychiatrist Dr W. J. Gray (1973), described it as 'an unique establishment ... attempting for the first time, in an English prison, a therapeutic approach to the treatment of non-psychotic recidivist offenders'.[10] As such the regime of Grendon differs from that of any other prison in that it revolves around therapy in the form of group discussions. There is no segregation unit for those who transgress against the rules, and yet for several years Grendon has seen the lowest numbers of offences against prison discipline.

Much of the controversy surrounding Grendon has concerned the seriousness of the offences committed by the people who go there, which has led to tabloid 'exposés' of the regime on offer. However, many of the prisoners believe it is the toughest regime in the entire prison system, because it requires them to confront their offending behaviour for the first time. Much of the academic debate about the establishment has centred on whether or not it works. In other words, does it help the 'non-psychotic recidivist offenders' to stop committing crime?

The first major study of the effectiveness of the Grendon regime was published in 1978; but it was inconclusive because it was based on reconviction rates, which were difficult to analyse and compare against a control group. A follow-up study nine years later claimed that Grendon was a 'catalyst, giving men who want to change the opportunity of spending their time in prison constructively'.[11]

More recently, in 1997, research into reconviction rates of those who went to Grendon has been able to show more clearly the effectiveness of the regime.[12] It considered just over 700 prisoners who had been

[10] Quoted in D. Wilson, 'Her Majesty's Prison Grendon: a maverick prison', *Journal of Forensic Psychiatry*, vol. 2, No. 2, September 1991, pp. 179–83.

[11] *ibid.*

[12] P. Marshall, *A reconviction study of the HMP Grendon therapeutic community*, London: HMSO, 1997.

admitted to Grendon between 1984 and 1989 and compared their reconviction rates with two 'control groups'. The results showed that ex-Grendon prisoners were less likely to be reconvicted than those on the waiting list who never got a chance to go there. Moreover, reconviction rates were lower for prisoners who stayed for longer periods at Grendon.

However, perhaps more telling than the research findings and statistics are the simple facts that in its entire history Grendon has had only one hostage incident, one escape and no major disturbances, despite the fact that it takes very violent offenders. Uniquely for a prison, it has a waiting list of around 200 prisoners who have volunteered to go there.

CONCLUSION

In this chapter a picture of the current prison situation has been presented. The picture is not very encouraging. There has been a dramatic increase in the number of offenders sent to prison, despite the fact that the majority of these tend to be non-violent offenders. The reconviction rates seem to demonstrate the futility of sending such people to prison, and it is our contention that better alternatives may exist for non-violent offenders than a custodial sentence. Of course, some offenders are considered a threat to public safety; they will continue to be imprisoned. If this is the case then more effort should be made to address their offending behaviour while in prison.

3 The Drive for Punishment: Fear of Crime and the Prison Economy

If sending more people to prison is expensive and counter-productive, why have recent governments adopted such policies? This chapter will attempt to answer the question. It will argue, first and foremost, that politicians have played up to a distorted fear of crime on the part of the public. But it will also examine the economic vested interests which, although still in their infancy in Britain, have played a worrying role in America's prison expansion.

PUBLIC CONCERN ABOUT CRIME

Crime is one of the most troubling aspects of contemporary life for the British public. A 1994 survey of 6,500 people found the British to be far more worried about crime than any of their European neighbours. Over half the British respondents (56 per cent) said that it was the issue that worried them most, compared with 13 per cent in Spain, 14 per cent in France, 37 per cent in Italy, and 43 per cent in Germany. According to the 1996 International Crime Victimisation Survey, nearly twice as many people in England and Wales believe that it is very likely that they will be burgled within the next 12 months than in any of the other 11 industrialised countries in the survey. This survey also found that England and Wales top the international league for expenditure on security devices, with more than 75 per cent of homes equipped with burglar alarms, reinforced door locks, protective grills on windows or doors, or steering wheel clamps. This compares with 42 per cent or less of homes in Austria, Sweden, Switzerland, Finland, and even Northern Ireland.

The BCS, which is generaly recognised as the most authoritative research into public attitiudes towards crime, found, in 1996, that 76 per cent of those polled believed that recorded crime had risen between 1993 and 1995, whereas it had in fact fallen slightly. Remarkably, 47 per cent believed that there had been a sharp rise in recorded crime.

This book would not have been written if there was not a growing crime problem in Britain, and it is not our intention to underplay the seriousness of the situation. However, it is also our belief that the public's understanding, in particular about violent crime, is part and parcel of the problem. It is violent crimes, such as assault, rape and murder, which, quite understandably, most concern the public. Yet the fears do not accord with reality. When an NOP poll asked a sample of the British public what proportion of crime they believed to be violent, the average response was 47 per cent, whereas the real figure is just 6 per cent. A 1995 BBC poll found that on average people believed that 26 per cent of the population would fall victim to violent crime over the following 12 months, yet the true figure is somewhere between 1 and 2 per cent. Seventy-eight per cent of those questioned for the 1996 BCS believed that over 30 per cent of crimes were violent, while only 3 per cent underestimated the level of violent crime.

Of the 6 per cent of crimes that are violent, 65 per cent are less serious, non life-threatening offences; and of the remainder, homicide and life-threatening offences account for just 6 per cent, robbery 19 per cent, and sexual offences 10 per cent.

According to the BCS, violent crime rose by around 21 per cent between 1981 and 1991, which is a significant rise but by no means an explosive one. The statistics recorded by the police show a sharper rise, but these figures should be treated with caution, because the reporting of some crimes, such as rape, has increased dramatically. Police officers and women's groups point out that in the not too distant past, many cases of sexual assault were not recorded or processed because police officers did not trust or believe the account given by the victim. There is general consensus that, in recent years, the police have become better at responding to the needs of victims of domestic violence and sexual offences and that, as a consequence, more victims are willing to come forward to report assaults.

The home is the most common setting for violence, with female and child family members being by far the most likely victims. Young men of between 16 and 24 are the main perpetrators of violence outside of the family, but they, rather than old ladies or young children, also account for the vast bulk of the victims.

The media and fear of crime

So how do we explain this distorted fear of crime? First we must look to the media.

The mainstream media, on the whole, do not aim to provide a pure reflection of the outside world, but rather to maximise their audiences and, in doing so, with the exception of publicly-owned institutions such as the BBC, maximise the profits of their owners. To attract audiences their products have to be entertaining, dramatic, exciting, and sometimes shocking. So, by virtue of the fact that crime can, depending on how it is presented, be all these things, it is ideal media fodder. The media cannot realistically be blamed for this — it is simply a fact of life.

At times crime seems like the life-blood of the television ratings, with everything from the real-life slapstick of 'Police Camera Action' to the finely crafted drama of 'Inspector Morse' attracting many millions of viewers. Television news, because of its immediacy, often appears to be presenting the world 'as it is', but it is not immune from the broader imperatives of the medium. News stories are picked, not only on the basis of their objective importance, but also according to how they will engage the interest of the viewers. A British serial killer who murders 10 people would generally be considered to be far more newsworthy than, say, a plane crash in Central Africa that kills 20 times as many.

Crime is, if anything, an even greater obsession for newspapers; indeed among the tabloids its only serious rivals are celebrity scandal and the royal family. A study of one month's news coverage by the national newspapers in 1989 found that almost 13 per cent was devoted to crime. For the tabloids the figure averaged over 22.5 per cent, and for the country's best selling daily newspaper, the *Sun*, it was over 30 per cent. It is a rare week indeed in which one of the tabloid newspapers does not have a crime story as its main front page splash, but in the battle for circulation the quality broadsheets are increasingly prepared to fill thousands of column inches with crime stories.

The obsession with violence

It is the type of crime that is covered, not just the vast quantity of that coverage, which is of such critical importance in stoking public fear of crime. A study of national newspapers from 1989 found that 60 per cent of the space devoted to crime reporting dealt with the tiny percentage of crimes involving serious personal violence. Local newspapers are little different. For example, a study of newspapers in Strathclyde in 1981 found that over 45 per cent of coverage was devoted to violent crimes, even though they constituted just 2.4 per cent of reported incidents. A similar study in Birmingham found that nearly 53 per cent of crime coverage concerned the 6 per cent of known crimes involving offences against the person.

Any news editor, whether in TV or in newspapers, will testify that a shocking violent crime story will attract viewers and readers in droves. A classic example would be a murder committed by a stranger, although, as we have seen, these crimes are also the rarest. The murder of a woman by her husband during a domestic dispute is unlikely to make the national news, precisely because such crimes are so much more common.

Highly graphic violent crime stories, with sensational headlines, embellished descriptions and lurid photos, can often have profound knock-on effects on public behaviour and opinion. For example, the murder of the Liverpool toddler James Bulger in 1993 by the 10-year-olds Robert Thompson and John Venables prompted many parents to stop their children venturing out onto the street unaccompanied. The fact that the abduction was recorded on closed circuit television finally silenced those who argued that there was a need to protect privacy and civil liberties from the intrusive use of video surveillance. The Bulger case helped clear the way for legislation that allowed children as young as 10 to be locked up, and reformed the common law presumption of '*doli incapax*' which presumed that a child under 14 did not know the difference between right and wrong (see below and Chapter 5). Yet there is no evidence that children are at any greater risk from such crimes than they have been previously. For example, in the 10 years up to 1992, just 10 children under the age of five were killed by strangers, as against 571 murdered by someone known to them (often the parents themselves). Murders of children by other children are even rarer, with only a handful of cases being recorded in the past 20 years.

Non-violent crimes can sometimes gain a high profile if there is an extraordinary angle to be exploited, but this too inevitably inflates the threat posed to the public. A classic example was the teenage burglar from the North East dubbed 'Rat boy', who hit the headlines in 1993–4. The 15-year-old, who had a string of convictions for burglary and managed to escape from various homes and secure units, acquired his name from his ability to evade the police by hiding in the ventilation shafts of one of Newcastle's housing estates. The newspaper feeding frenzy triggered by the story sometimes gave the impression that there was a 'Rat boy' around every corner and that no pensioner's house was safe.

Media bandwagons and moral panics

In all probability the 'Rat boy' story would not have had such widespread coverage were it not for the fact that it came during a rash of media stories suggesting that the problem of juvenile crime was getting out of hand. As media bandwagons go, the problem of out-of-control children was particularly effective in influencing Government policy (see below), but it was by no means the first of its kind. When it was revealed that one of James Bulger's killers may have watched a video of 'Childs Play 3', a major debate took place on the effects of screen violence on the young. Certain newspapers and MPs demanded tighter censorship laws, yet there was little or no evidence that screen violence alone could influence behaviour.

In the late 1980s, coverage of drunken brawls in prosperous towns across the Home Counties, led to the coining of the phrase 'lager lout'. For a while any lager lout story was almost guaranteed tabloid exposure, which gave the impression that respectable middle England was under seige from a new menace. In fact there was nothing to suggest that anything more dramatic was happening than one of the periodic increases of drunken violence that occur during times of relative prosperity, when people have more disposable income to spend on drink.

In the 1970s, the media fuelled a moral panic about 'mugging' — a supposedly new form of street crime that had been imported from the United States. A judge at Birmingham Crown Court was prompted to pass an 'exemplary' sentence of 20 years' detention against a 16-year-old mugger from the city. Despite the intention of the judge, this does not seem to have deterred a rise in street robberies. Mugging remains one of the most feared street crimes in Britain, yet it does not appear on police records or in the official criminal statistics because it does not have a separate crime classification. There is therefore no way of knowing if scare stories about mugging being on the increase are true.

During the 1960s, media coverage of the pitched battles between Mods and Rockers at seaside resorts created a similar moral panic about the permissive society, but, contrary to the prophecies of some contemporary commentators, society did not implode. Indeed, such behaviour was commonplace during the late Victorian period, which is all too often portrayed as a golden age of strict public morality. During the August Bank Holiday weekend of 1898, for example, there was a series of clashes between gangs of youths from the East End of London and the police. Football hooliganism was also quite common. Yet to read most present-day newspaper coverage, one could be forgiven for believing it to be an phenomenon of the last 30 years.

Ironically, the Victorian press was no less prone to starting moral bandwagons than its present-day descendants. One of the most interesting early examples is the 1862 'garroting panic', a largely forgotten episode which contains many contemporary resonances about 'law 'n' order'.[1] In July 1862, Hugh Pilkington MP was attacked and robbed on Pall Mall as he was walking to the Reform Club. He was attacked from behind, and temporarily lost consciousness as a result of being choked or 'garroted'. A number of similar robberies were thereafter reported, which provoked a sustained press campaign demanding action against the perpetrators. The *Manchester Guardian*, for example, declared on 2 November 1862:

> Under the influence of our humanity-mongers, we have nursed and fostered a race of hardened villains ... well the public is now learning, in a rather startling fashion, what is the natural result of making pets of thieves and garroters.[2]

The impact on public opinion

Because the news is primarily concerned with the immediate (news is, after all, the plural of 'new'), its crime coverage naturally focuses, first

---

[1] For a full account of the garroting panic see J. Sharpe, 'Crime, Order, and Historical Change', in J. Muncie and E. McLaughlin (eds), *The Problem of Crime*, London: Sage, 1996, pp. 101–41.

[2] Sharpe (1996), p. 138.

and foremost, on the criminal acts themselves. It is less concerned with the underlying causes and the measures that might be taken to stop such crimes occurring in the future. Increasingly the coverage also focuses on the far-reaching and long-term impact of the offence on the victims and their families, and this has fuelled demands that politicians and the criminal justice system protect the rights of victims rather than those of the offenders.

The wholly understandable popular response to the mainstream media's representation of society as an increasingly violent and dangerous place is to demand 'tough' action against the offender. The 14th Public Attitudes Survey, published in November 1997, found that 70 per cent of those polled believed that criminals deserve tougher sentences, and 86 per cent believed that too many of those convicted are let off lightly.

The 1996 BCS found that an overwhelming 79 per cent of the 16,000 people polled thought that the courts were too lenient, with 51 per cent believing them to be much too lenient. Eighty-two per cent thought that judges were out of touch, and 63 per cent believed the same applied to magistrates. Crucially, the survey suggested that it was in fact the public who were out of touch with sentencing practice. When asked what proportion of adult male rapists, burglars and muggers got prison sentences, the majority underestimated by over 30 per cent. The correct imprisonment figures for 1995 were 97 per cent for rapists, 61 per cent for burglars, and between 60 and 80 per cent for muggers; but the people polled thought that the figure was less than 60 per cent of rapists, under a third of burglars, and under 45 per cent of muggers.

Perhaps the most interesting — and certainly the most ironic — finding of the survey was that, despite their belief that the courts were too lenient, if sentencing decisions were left to the public they might be no more punitive than judges, and possibly less so. Those polled were given details of an actual case in which a burglary, involving the theft of a video, had been committed in the daytime by a person with previous convictions, and where the victim was an elderly man who was out at the time. They were then asked to say what sentence they would have expected. Fifty-four per cent suggested a prison term, with sentence lengths averaging less than two years, whereas in the actual case the offender was given a two-year sentence.

Politicians play on the fear of crime

The public cannot be blamed for their misconceptions about crime and sentencing. The real problem is that politicians have shown themselves ever more willing to play along with those misconceptions. No one understands how public perceptions are shaped better than politicians; indeed, so much of modern politics is played out via TV studios and lobby briefings that it is impossible to consider politics and the media in isolation from each other. It is, after all, a rare media bandwagon that has not been pushed along by politicians.

However, this is not a phenomenon of the late 20th century. The 1862 garroting panic, for example, led to the passing of the Security from Violence Act, which amongst many changes re-introduced the use of corporal punishment for adult offenders. This in turn paved the way for the Penal Servitude Act 1865 and the appointment of the hard-liner, Sir Edmund du Cane, as the first Chairman of the Directors of Convict Prisons in 1869. It was also du Cane who was later to maintain that the purpose of imprisonment was to punish and deter.

The pattern is familiar: a violent crime is committed and, depending upon its newsworthiness, gets publicity, which in turn can become a concerted campaign for action, or perhaps just punishment. This campaign attracts political support, which in turn involves mobilising the police, the courts and the penal system to counteract this new threat to the community. This approach is sometimes called the 'politics of law and order'.

The Conservative Party has generally profited the most from the politics of law and order and the public attitudes described above, which underpin them. The party's 'common-sense' view, that crime is purely the responsibility of the offender and that punishment should be both retribution and a deterrent to others, is far easier to get across to the public via the media than the traditional liberal or left-wing analyses, which consider the wider social and economic forces which are beyond the individual's control. Hardly surprising, then, that the old Labour Party was portrayed as 'soft' on crime and that the Conservatives were able to pursue the law and order issue to their own advantage, particularly during Margaret Thatcher's first election campaign in 1979.

As we have seen in Chapter 1, though, for all Mrs Thatcher's tough talk on crime, her party did not adopt the hard-line law and order policies of her fellow neo-Conservatives in the USA until Michael Howard became Home Secretary in 1993, three years after she had been replaced as leader by John Major. The media and distorted fears about violent crime each played a central role in affecting that shift, and in the subsequent scramble by the two main political parties to portray themselves as the guardians of law and order.

It was the Labour Party which started the process. Smarting from their fourth successive general election defeat in April 1992, the leadership took some comfort from the victory later that year in the US presidential election of Democratic candidate, Bill Clinton.

Clinton was well aware of the role that media presentations of crime played in the failure of the previous Democratic presidential contender Michael Dukakis. Dukakis had enjoyed a lead in the polls over the Republican nominee George Bush; but the public mood had shifted decisively against him, in large measure through a TV advertising campaign which reminded viewers that during his tenure as Governor of Massachusetts it was state policy to allow home leave for convicted felons, and that one of these convicts, Willie Horton, had used the opportunity to commit a rape. (The advertisement also cynically played the race card: Horton was black and his victim was white.)

Determined not to fall prey to similar negative campaigning, Clinton demonstrated that he was tough on crime in his 1992 presidential bid by scheduling the execution of a brain-damaged man shortly before the crucial New Hampshire primary election. Indeed, Clinton himself left the campaign trail to return to Arkansas, where he was State Governor, to preside over the execution of Rickey Ray Rector, a black man sentenced to death by an all-white jury. Rector had destroyed part of his brain when he turned the murder weapon on himself. This helps to explain why prison records show that on the days leading up to the execution, Rector was found howling and barking like a dog, singing and dancing, laughing inappropriately and claiming that he was going to vote for Clinton. On eating his final meal, he stated, without being ironic, that he was leaving his dessert 'for later'.[3]

Once elected to office, Clinton proved as tough as he had promised to be. The prison population continued to rocket, and by 1994 had reached 1,544,000. He introduced a series of hard-line federal laws, most famously 'three strikes and you're out', which required federal

---

[3] S. Bright and P. Keenan, 'Judges and the Politics of Death: Deciding between the Bill of Rights and the Next Election in Capital Cases', *Boston University Law Review*, vol. 75, No. 3, May 1995.

courts to hand down mandatory life sentences to people convicted of their third felony. The measure was first introduced in California at the initiative of Governor Pete Wilson and is perhaps the most notorious example of pandering to simplistic public opinion. It was dreamed up not by criminologists, but by a public relations company hired by Wilson's political campaign team, who calculated that the public would understand an idea borrowed from the national sport of baseball far better than it would a complex judicial principle. The legislation has resulted in some horrific cases, such as that of Michael Garcia, an unemployed heroin addict who received a 25-year sentence for stealing meat worth less than $6. The court had no choice in sentencing Garcia because he had already been convicted twice of felonies. The fact that his earlier convictions involved only small sums of money and that he had not caused anyone injury was of no relevance; neither was the fact that the meat was to feed his retarded brother and his mother, whose social security payment was late. In the 1996 presidential election, Clinton's first three TV advertisements all focused on crime and his support for expanding the death penalty. He thus presented himself from the outset as the 'tough on law and order' candidate.

The Labour Party stayed in close contact with Bill Clinton's successful election team and learned much about their slick polling and presentational skills. They were aware that they could exploit the growth in crime under the Conservatives to their own electoral advantage, as long as they shed their media image as being soft on crime. The party's fastest rising young star, Shadow Home Secretary Tony Blair, came up with a slogan 'tough on crime, tough on the causes of crime' which could be easily digested by the media and would appeal to conservative Middle England, without alienating too many of the party's traditional socialist supporters. Blair's new moral crusade undoubtedly struck a chord in the wake of the James Bulger murder when many public figures and media commentators were suggesting that the nation was on the brink of a moral abyss.

When he became Home Secretary in 1993, Michael Howard must have known that, despite its new posturing, Labour remained squeamish about US-style criminal justice policies, hence the calculated political gamble of his 1993 conference 'prison works' speech (see Chapters 1 and 2). His promise shortly afterwards to put victims at the centre of criminal justice policies was a clear reaction to the growth of the victim movement.

As we have seen, Howard's 'prison works' initiative increased the prison population of England and Wales by around 50 per cent in just four years. But the vast majority of the prison boom was not accounted for by the 'murderers, muggers and rapists' whom Howard referred to in the same sound bite from his conference speech, but by non-violent offenders.

Howard's tough policies were not enough to rescue the Conservative Party from its landslide electoral defeat of 1 May 1997, but the 14th British Social Attitudes Survey, published seven months after the election, confirmed that he had tapped into a vein of popular feeling. As an article in *The Times* commented on 19 November 1997: 'The [survey's] conclusions suggest that Jack Straw, the Home Secretary, has little option other than to follow the tough line taken by his predecessor, Michael Howard, if he is to retain public support.'

Jack Straw was well aware of the public mood. In opposition, although he was looking to score points against Michael Howard at every available opportunity, he fought shy of promising to reverse the 'prison works' policies. Indeed, as the general election approached, he explicitly stated that under the coming Labour Government the prison population would probably continue to rise. There were also promises to lock up persistent young offenders under the age of 14 in five new secure training centres, to introduce US-style zero tolerance policing to the streets of our cities and, most famously, to crack down on aggressive beggars and 'squeegee merchants'. Labour supported Howard's Crime (Sentences) Act, the last major piece of legislation to be passed before the election, which, by introducing mandatory minimum sentences and other measures, was expected to expand the prison population by a further 10,700.

Since coming to office Jack Straw has continued to be populist, talk tough and, as we have seen, the prison population has continued to rise. Nevertheless, through its proposals for an extension of electronic tagging and the early release of prisoners, his flagship Crime and Disorder Bill, announced in December 1997, promises to cut the prison population by 10 per cent. The Bill also promises measures to steer young offenders away from a life of crime and imprisonment. It does, however, include a series of Draconian proposals, such as the abolition of the ancient legal principle of *doli incapax*, and the introduction of powers that will allow courts to remand children over the age of 12 to secure accommodation. There can be little doubt that these measures were largely a response to the over-inflated media coverage of juvenile crime. Indeed, it is quite likely that his plans to criminalise 10-year-olds would have caused uproar were it not for the fact that the media had gone over, in fine detail, what two 10-year-olds had done to James Bulger (see above).

The Government would argue that, in extending training to the young unemployed and prioritising education, it is also making good its promise to be 'tough on the causes of crime'. It is too early to judge the success of these initiatives, but, as we argue in Chapter 2 and elsewhere, as long as the Government continues to pander to distorted public fears about crime, its criminal justice policies will be doomed to failure.

THE PRISON ECONOMY

The American experience

Crime-obsessed media and opportunistic politicians have each played their role in fuelling the prison explosion. There is also another factor which, although it has so far hardly reared its head in Britain, we ignore at our peril. To understand it we need to look once again at the USA, where the trebling of the prison population since the early 1980s has unleashed a powerful amalgamation of economic and commercial forces which have a vested interest in pushing those numbers still higher.[4] It has been dubbed the 'prison–industrial complex' because of its similarities to the military–industrial complex which dominated US foreign policy during the Cold War.

When he coined the term in the 1950s, President Eisenhower was referring to the 'iron triangle' of the defence industry, politicians and government bureaucracy. For its survival the defence industry relied on huge defence spending by the Government. The Government in turn recognised that this spending was in its own interests because the industry provided, on the one hand, vast numbers of jobs and, on the other, the hardware necessary to maintain the country's defences against the Soviet Union.

In the prison–industrial complex the prisons take the role of the defence manufacturers and the criminal replaces the Russian Bear. The

---

[4] The account of developments in the United States follows that provided by S. R. Donziger (ed), *The Real War on Crime*, New York: Harper Collins, 1996.

problem, say critics, is that in order to safeguard jobs and profits, the threat of crime (like the threat of global communism before it) is overplayed.

Although the analogy may seem far-fetched, it is anything but. Over the past 20 years, US Government spending on crime control has increased at more than double the rate of defence spending. The $100b it now spends annually on law enforcement, together with the $65b spent on private security, almost matches the Pentagon's annual defence budget. Furthermore, the defence industry is getting in on the act, with some of the largest companies establishing departments solely dedicated to adapting their hi-tech military products to civilian law enforcement. The hardware goes on show at conferences co-sponsored by the Department of Justice and private industry organisations like the American Defence Preparedness Association.

At the pinnacle of the 'iron triangle' is the new private correctional industry. Today there are over 90 private prisons housing around 80,000 prisoners. Although this represents only around 3 per cent of the total US prison population, it should be remembered that only 15 years ago there were no private prisons at all. The industry continues to grow apace, and market analysts predict that its revenues will pass $2b by the end of the decade.

The market leader in private prisons is the Corrections Corporation of America (CCA). Founded in 1983, by the end of 1996 it had a 49 per cent share of America's private prisons market. In February 1998 it had 52,890 beds in 67 facilities, mainly in the USA, but also in Australia, Puerto Rico and the UK (see below). In 1997 the company opened 15,000 beds, which, according to its Chairman and Chief Executive Officer, Dr R. Crants, is 'more than any corrections system, public or private, has ever opened in a single year'.[5] The company's net profit after tax in 1997 was $53.9m, up from $30.9m the previous year. According to *Fortune* magazine, it is now one of America's 100 fastest growing businesses.

CCA's founders and board of directors include people with high-level establishment connections, including T. Don Hutto, a former Commissioner of Corrections for Arkansas and Virginia, and Thomas Beasley, former chair of the Tennessee Republican Party. In 1993 the company appointed to the position of Director of Strategic Planning Mike

---

[5] CCA press release, 19 February 1998.

Quinlan, who had spent the previous five years as Director of the Federal Bureau of Prisons.

Given these political ties, companies like CCA have inevitably been accused of lobbying for still tougher law and order policies and a further expansion of the prison population. The company denies this and points out that its growth targets can be met by taking over existing publicly run prisons. Quinlan, who is a highly respected bureaucrat with comparatively liberal views on law and order, has even said publicly that he would like to see the overall prison population reduce in size. The 1994 Federal Crime Bill, which allocated $9.7b for prison construction, was, nevertheless, described by the company's financial officer as 'very favourable to us'.

The private prison companies are not the only ones to benefit from America's prison boom. The prison industry's trade magazine, *Corrections Today*, has seen a threefold increase in the advertising of prison products since 1980. A poster for the American Jail Association's 1995 annual convention entreated the companies who attended to 'tap into the $65 billion local jails market' and reminded them 'Jails are BIG BUSINESS'. Everyone, from architects and builders, through to catering companies and protective clothing manufacturers, is jumping on the bandwagon. The health care market alone is currently worth $3b pa, and that figure is set to rise as longer sentences create ever-larger numbers of older prisoners requiring medical services. Correctional Medical Services of St Louis now looks after 150,000 inmates, which is a threefold increase in a decade.

The growth of the correctional industry has been paralleled by the growth of organised labour. By 1992, almost 525,000 people were employed in correctional facilities in the US — more than the workforce of every major American company with the exception of General Motors. Prison officers are organised on a state by state basis, and many state organisations make no secret of their aggressive political lobbying for measures that have increased the prison population. The most powerful and active of all is the California Correctional Peace Officers Association, whose membership grew from 4,000 to 23,000 in a decade. With $8m a year raised in dues, it has become the second largest campaign donor in the state, spending around $1m pa backing political candidates who favour prison expansion. The union reckons that an astonishing 38 out of the 44 bills that it backed were enacted by the California state legislature. Predictably one of its largest financial contributions went to the campaign to support the 'three strikes and you're out' initiative when the proposed legislation went to a ballot in 1992.

Private industry and organised labour are undoubtedly potent forces behind the growth of the prison-industrial complex, but there is another, more insidious, economic process at work. American communities, many still ravaged by the decline in traditional industries and agriculture, are increasingly coming to see prisons as a short-cut to economic growth. Until a few years ago the building of a prison in an American town was likely to trigger vociferous local objection, but now communities are lining up to attract prisons. In Texas, for example, some towns bombarded the state's Department of Criminal Justice with incentives such as country club membership for prison wardens. In one of the towns a Sunday school class actually got on their knees and prayed that a prison would be built locally. In Minnesota, the community of Appleton, whose population is just 1,500, issued bonds worth $28.5m to build a prison, even though it did not have a commitment that the cells would be needed.

Whatever fears people may have had about having a prison in their midst tend to be outweighed by other considerations. As the California Department of Corrections' Chief of Prison Construction, Ernie Van Sant, put it: 'We are not an industrial developer. We don't use a lot of chemicals. We're somewhat recession-proof.' The experience of some small communities has, however, been far from happy. Many of the new jobs go to outsiders who either commute or, if they live locally, often force up property prices and change the character of the community. There also is, frequently, an influx of prisoners' families, which in turn strains the local welfare and education services. Existing residents in some towns have complained that the families are responsible for increased social problems and crime.

The private sector in Britain

Private companies already have a substantial interest in our prison system.[6] The Criminal Justice Act 1991 provided for the contracting out of prison escort services and the private management of new prisons

---

[6] We are grateful to Stephen Nathan of the Prison Reform Trust who edits *Prison Privatisation Report International* for the information provided in this section.

holding unsentenced prisoners. The Act was extended in 1992 to allow the private management of new prisons containing convicted prisoners, and again in 1993 to allow existing prisons to be privately managed. So far no existing prisons have gone private, but four new ones are privately run and two of the companies involved are part-owned by the largest players in America's private corrections industry. Table 8 shows the existing foothold established by the private sector in Britain.

Prison	Opened	Contracator
The Wolds	1992	Group 4
Blakenhurst	1993	UKDS[8]
Doncaster	1993	Premier Prisons[9]
Buckley Hall	1994	Group 4
Parc[10]	1997	Securicor
Altcourse[10]	1997	Group 4
Lowdham Grange[10]	1998	Premier Prisons
Agecroft (Salford)[10]	1999	UKDS
Pucklechurch (Bristol)[10]	1999	Premier Prisons
Marchington (E. Staffs)[10]	1999	To be Announced
Secure Training Centre Cookham Wood[10, 11]	1998	Group 4
HMP Coldingley[12]	1998	Wackenhut (UK) Ltd

Table 8   Private Prisons in England and Wales[7]

In 1993, the East Midlands and Humberside region became the first whose court escort service was privatised. Despite a very shaky start — which saw a number of prisoners escape while they were supposedly being guarded by Group 4 personnel — most other regions' services have since been privatised.

[7] There are 3 private prisons planned in Scotland.

[8] UKDS is a joint partnership of CCA and Sodexho.

[9] Premium Prisons is jointly owned by Wackenhut and Serio Plc.

[10] These prisons are design, construct, manage and financed (DCMF) which means they have a contract for 25 years.

[11] For 12–14 year olds only.

[12] Industries only.

The details of the contracts between the Home Office and private operators are supposed to be confidential, on the grounds of their commercial sensitivity, but in 1994 the Prison Reform Trust used America's freedom of information system to obtain documents relating to UK prison contracts that the Corrections Corporation of America and Wakenhut had filed with the US Securities and Exchange Commission. The documents revealed that both companies expected their UK prisons (the CCA's Blakenhurst and Wakenhut's Doncaster) to cost about £10m during their first year of operation. Among other things, Wakenhut documents included a schedule of the key performance indicators contained in the contract. It was agreed that there would be:

No more than two escapes from prison by the end of the first year of operation, thereafter no more than one in each year; no more than eight escapes from escort in each of the first three years and no more than six in the fourth year; no more than 77 assaults on staff by the end of the first year; no more than 148 assaults on prisoners by other prisoners in the first year. If these figures are reached then financial penalties could be incurred.

In 1993 the Government agreed a strategy for 10 per cent of prisons to become privately managed, including all the new ones and a selection of existing ones. It was believed that these plans would be unlikely to be enacted under the Labour administration, but, despite voicing its ideological opposition to private prisons, the Government now refuses to move the four new prisons back into the public sector and has extended prisons privatisation.

Labour endorsement of the previous Government's Private Finance Initiative, which aims to stimulate private business partnerships with the public sector, is likely to result in further profit being made from Britain's prison boom. The Home Office is looking to the PFI as a means for providing the new jails required to absorb the estimated increase of 10,700 in the prison population which is expected to result from Michael Howard's 1997 Crime (Sentences) Act, and the private sector has been invited to 'design, build and manage' more prisons. Contracts have already been drawn up with Tarmac to build the five proposed secure training centres for children under the age of 14, and the first contract has been let to Group 4 for the Secure Training Centre at Cookham Wood.

In 1995 the Conservative Government hired the accountancy firm Coopers & Lybrand to examine other areas of the prison service suitable for an extension of private sector involvement. A number of projects were identified, including prison refurbishment, catering, prison workshops, CCTV systems and information technology.

An example of how all of this works in practice within Britain is the development of Group 4's interests in prisons and prison related businesses. Group 4 Prison Services Ltd is a wholly owned subsidiary of Prison and Court Services Ltd, which, in turn is a subsidiary of Group 4 Securitas NV which is registered in the Netherlands Antilles. The ultimate parent company of Group 4 Securitas NV is Secom Investments II NV, which is also incorporated in the Netherlands Antilles. On the parent company's Management Board is Jim Harrower, who is also executive vice president of Group 4 Securitas Ltd, and a director of 29 other companies including Group 4 Court Services Ltd, Group 4 Tarmac (Fazakerley) Ltd; Fazakerley Prison Services Ltd; Rebound ECD Ltd and the British Security Industry Association. Rebound ECD Ltd won the contract to run the Secure Training Centre at Cookham Wood, and subsequently Group 4 has now set up another company ECD (Cookham Wood) Ltd. Seemingly ECD stands for Education, Care and Discipline.[13]

It is always difficult to establish how much money is generated out of prisons, and businesses associated with prisons, but clearly there is profit to be made. Premier Prison Services Ltd made a pre-tax operating profit of £1.1m on income from the Prison Service of £18.4m in the year ended 31 December 1996. The company also earned a further £127,442 on investments. Securicor Custodial Services Ltd, which has prisoner escort and tagging contracts, and recently won the contract to run HMP Parc, made a pre-tax opeating profit of just under £1m on income from the Prison Service of £21.97m. UKDS, which runs HMP Blakenhurst made a pre-tax operating profit of just under £.5m and paid a dividend of £600,000 to its share holders CCA (UK) Ltd. Group 4 Prison Services Ltd received £12.29m from the Prison Service in the year ended December 1996, and declared a pre-tax operating profit of £169,000.[14]

Group 4 will be hoping to do better with their contract to run the Secure Training Centre at Cookham Wood. The costs are certainly steep.

---

[13] See Prison Report, Issue No. 41 (Winter) 1997, p. 15.
[14] All figures taken from Prison Report, Issue No. 41 (Winter) 1997, p. 14.

Each child locked up in a Secure Training Centre will cost £250,000 per annum, or £4,800 per week, which is more expensive than staying at the Ritz Hotel. Cookham Wood has space for 40 children.[15]

Could it happen here?

In Britain the proposed building of a new prison almost always arouses deep local hostility, and there are no signs, so far, of communities actively lobbying to attract prisons. Perhaps the British are culturally too different from the Americans to ever regard the warehousing of fellow humans as a means of economic survival. But we should not be complacent. Not so long ago many Americans were similarly squeamish, yet the culture shift happened at breakneck speed. In 1984, for example, 23 state prison departments reported local opposition to prison building, but by 1988 that number had fallen to just five, with 24 states reporting no opposition whatsoever.

In recent years in Britain, forward-looking local authorities have fallen over themselves to attract 'clean' new businesses such as electronics manufacturers and out-of-town supermarkets. It may not be long before enterprising economic development officers in town halls across the country begin to look to prisons as a means of providing their locality with hundreds of recession-proof jobs.

---

[15] Prison Privatisation Report International, No. 16, January 1998, p. 5.

4   Young People and Crime

Last year one of our committee attended a parents' evening at the local school in London where her eldest son is educated, and where she and her husband intend to send their youngest boy. The headmistress opened the evening with a talk. She began not by outlining the school's attitude towards uniforms, or by describing the school's facilities, but by explaining the school's policy on exclusions: 'We will do everything we can to help,' she assured her audience, 'but make no mistake, if your son or daughter gets into trouble, they *will* be excluded.' This statement received thunderous applause. Children, you see — especially other people's children — are trouble.

This is a view that has rapidly gained ground in recent years. Quite naturally there is widespread public concern about the extent of youth crime, which intensified in the wake of the murder of James Bulger by two 10-year-old boys. The tabloid press, and on occasions the police, have been particularly keen to draw attention to young children who they claim are out of control but untouched by the courts. Our criminal justice system has attempted to respond to this concern through prosecutions, convictions and sentencing, and new tough measures are announced almost daily. New Labour's response, for example, has been to propose, consider or experimentally trial a variety of measures, some of which have appeared in their flagship Crime and Disorder Bill, which the Home Secretary has described as 'the biggest shake-up for 50 years in tackling juvenile crime'.[1] We can only be grateful that Mr Straw hasn't proposed bringing back the birch or National Service.

It is our belief that New Labour's approach is too narrowly focused, and that in particular these new 'tough' measures have little chance of success in reducing offending and may even in some circumstances make matters worse. Rather, we believe in, and will outline in this chapter, measures which will reduce youth crime by concentrating on prevention, supporting families, helping schools to reduce truancy and exclusions, and increasing leisure and training opportunities for young people. At the heart of this approach is our commitment to value our young people as this country's greatest resource, as opposed to the human equivalent of dangerous dogs.

THE PROBLEM OF YOUTH CRIME

What's the trouble with kids today?

The youth crime problem is, arguably, *the* crime problem. The peak age of offending is 18 for males and 15 for females and the vast majority of career criminals start when they are teenagers. It should be remembered that no one really knows the true extent of crime committed by either the young or the old in our country, but according to Home Office statistics, 43 per cent of 'indictable' crime — which means that these charges are usually heard at a Crown Court — seems to be committed by people under 21, and 26 per cent by under-18s. The most common crimes of young people in this age group are theft and handling stolen goods.[2]

A self-report study by the Home Office about young people and crime would also suggest that offending is quite common amongst young people.[3] In any given year, evidence from this study suggests that a sizeable number of young people will commit an offence, usually buying or selling stolen goods, fighting, vandalism or shoplifting. In its report *Misspent Youth*, the Audit Commission estimated that youth crime costs public services £1b each year.[4]

---

[1] Quoted in the *Guardian*, 26 September 1997.

[2] All figures quoted are taken from NACRO (1997), p. 9.

[3] J. Graham and B. Bowling, Young People and Crime, Home Office Research Study 145, London: HMSO, 1995.

[4] Audit Commission, Misspent Youth ... Young People and Crime, London: Audit Commission, 1996.

These figures are undoubtedly worrying, but it is also evident that most young offenders commit only one or two, mostly minor, crimes, and that to have the criminal justice system intervene against them would be costly and counter-productive. There is also evidence that, contrary to the impression given by the tabloid press, the problem of youth crime may actually have decreased.

The reported rate of offending among young people in the age group 14–17 has fallen from 8,142 per 100,000 in 1985 to 6,468 in 1995; and despite what we are assured of in the tabloid press, it has also fallen among 10–13-year-old males, from 3,231 per 100,000 in 1985 to 1,605 per 100,000 in 1995. Despite some fluctuations, there have been similar falls for young girls, from 1,048 per 100,000 for 10–13-year-olds in 1985 to 687 per 100,000 in 1995. As a consequence of these falls there has been a sharp decrease in the recorded number of juvenile offenders. In the past decade the number of male juvenile offenders has fallen by 41 per cent, from 172,700 in 1985 to 101,700 in 1995; and the number of females has fallen by 24 per cent from 40,700 in 1985 to 31,000 in 1995. Lastly, according to statistics produced by NACRO, nearly 60 per cent of offenders aged between 16 and 17 were unemployed on the date of their sentence.

These figures are in many ways controversial, as they conflict with our knowledge that both the recorded crime statistics and the BCS show that crime has substantially increased in the last 40 years. The fall in the rate of known offending may be due to demographic changes, which means that there were fewer teenagers in 1995 than in 1985, or it may be that more young offenders are getting away with their crimes.

We believe that it is helpful to try to distinguish different groups of young offenders, as opposed to believing that every young person who commits an offence is 'out of control' and a menace to society. By grouping young offenders in this way, we will be in a better position to judge what our response should be to these young people, as each group will have different needs, requirements and prognoses.[5]

---

[5] See, for example, the speech given by Prof. Spencer Millham of the Dartington Social Research Unit, entitled 'Social Policy and Young Offenders: The Lessons from Research', delivered at the Queen Elizabeth II Conference Centre, 5 March 1995. We use Prof. Millham's categorisation of young offender groups.

Types of young offenders

The first, and probably largest, group of young offenders can be described as *temporary delinquents*. These youngsters merely experiment with crime, which is usually of a very minor nature and committed in the company of other young people. The rewards are usually small, and it is rare for young people in this group to continue in crime. If caught, this type of young offender is usually discouraged by a police caution (see evidence from the 'Milton Keynes Retail Theft Initiative' below) even if no further action is taken.

The second group can be called *difficult and disturbed*. Their involvement in crime might also be temporary, but their offending has to be seen within a wider context of other problems, which are likely to require the use of a care or supervision order, perhaps for a long period of time. However, there is little evidence to suggest that incarceration and tougher responses will deal effectively with the problems associated with this group of offenders. In this respect we are impressed by the Scottish children's panel system, which we describe below.

A third, much smaller group can be described as comprising *one-off serious offenders* . This group will commit murder, manslaughter, arson, rape or other violent crimes. The offence often happens with little or no indication of there being anything 'wrong' (although problems often emerge later) and usually results in a lengthy period of detention. Evidence suggests that less than 20 per cent of *one-off serious offenders* who go to youth treatment centres became involved again in an offence which involves physical contact; and only two out of 104 such young offenders, who have been part of a follow-up study, committed another serious offence.[6]

A fourth group involves *persistent serious offenders*, and children in this group have a much poorer chance of staying free from crime. However, there are very few youngsters who fall into this category, although actual numbers will depend on the definition we use for 'persistent', which we describe shortly. Some measure of how many children fall into this category can be gauged from the numbers in youth treatment centres who have been convicted of murder or attempted murder. Youth treatment centres were set up in the 1970s, in the wake of the case of Mary Bell, an 11-year-old girl who was convicted of

---

[6] Outlined in Millham's speech, p. 10.

murdering two infants in 1968 and who has again become notorious with the publication of a biography on her, for which she received payment. Until the murder of James Bulger in 1993 there were only eight children under the age of 15 accommodated in youth treatment centres, convicted of murder or attempted murder.

The last group comprises *persistent young offenders* who (with the previous group) generate most of the attention of the media and politicians. Lord Bingham, the Lord Chief Justice, for example, in his otherwise admirable speech to the Prison Reform Trust last year, claimed that 'there is a small but identifiable core of young offenders whose criminal conduct is such as to call for serious punitive sentences'.[7] While it is undoubtedly true that there is likely to be a small group of young people who will refuse to be deflected from crime, there are very loose definitions of what 'persistent' means. This in turn makes it difficult to identify who is included in this group and how we should best respond to them.

A Home Office research study by Tim Newburn and Ann Hagell,[8] about the nature and extent of persistent young offenders, looked, amongst other things, at the question of how to define 'persistence' and at the consequences of making different definitions. In essence the authors wanted to discover if there was a small group of young people who, because of their criminal behaviour, accounted for a disproportionate amount of crime. They also wanted to discover — if this group actually existed — what sort of backgrounds these children had.

By using three different definitions of persistence — (i) frequency of offending over 12 months; (ii) offending over a three-month period; and (iii) the criteria for the proposed new secure training orders — the project discovered only 531 juveniles who had been arrested at least three times in 1992. The offences of children in this group reflected the usual range of juvenile crime, and the most frequent crimes related to road traffic offences, car theft, criminal damage, and non-residential burglary. Significantly the authors concluded that 'there was no evidence of the existence of offenders, and often portrayed by the media, having hundreds of convictions or known offences'.[9] Neither did the study discover a small number of offenders accounting for an extremely

---

[7] Lord Bingham of Cornhill, *Justice for the Young*, London: PRT, 1997, p. 14.

[8] T. Newburn and A. Hagell, *Persistent Young Offenders*, Home Office Research Bulletin 37, London: HMSO, 1995.

[9] *ibid.*, (1995), p. 19.

large proportion of crime. In short, very few frequent re-offenders were identified, and fewer still whose frequent offending continued over an extended period to time.

WHAT CAUSES YOUTH CRIME?

A research study which followed the lives of 411 boys born in 1956 to adulthood discovered that the major risk factors associated with youth crime are:

- low school attainment
- low income/poor housing
- a high degree of impulsiveness
- poor parental supervision/ harsh or erratic discipline
- parental conflict with broken families.[10]

Common sense tells us that, while the causes of youth crime are as broad and complex as the causes of all crime, education (or lack of it), plays a central role. The research of Tim Newburn and Ann Hagell, for example, found that the small number of young people who re-offended usually had high levels of truancy, disruptive classroom behaviour, school suspensions and exclusions.

Seventy per cent of young offenders are either regular truants, or have been excluded from school. The 1991 National Prisoners Survey, for example, found that 45 per cent of prisoners had left school before the age of 16, including 1 per cent who said that they had never attended school, whereas only 11 per cent of the general population under 25 left school before 16.[11] When the Basic Skills Agency carried out in-depth interviews with 500 young offenders between the ages of 17 and 25, it found that 21 per cent could not write their names and addresses without error, and 48 per cent could not give more than two further pieces of information about themselves without making mistakes. Only 30 per cent were capable of filling in a job application form satisfactorily. Sixty-four per cent reported that they were habitual truants, and 55 per cent said that they had committed crimes while traunting. These findings

---

[10] Quoted in NACRO (1997), p. 12.

[11] Quoted in NACRO, *A New Three Rs for Young Offenders: Towards a New Strategy for Children who Offend*, London: NACRO, 1997, p. 17.

were confirmed by the Metropolitan Police Commissioner, Sir Paul Condon, who reported to the Government that children between 10 and 16 are responsible for 40 per cent of all street robberies and a third of all car thefts, mostly while truanting.[12]

Many factors contribute to educational failing, but the reforms of the education system introduced over the past decade have undoubtedly exacerbated the problem. League tables have given schools an incentive to exclude pupils who might jeopardise their league placing. It is surely no coincidence that exclusions have increased fourfold since the introduction of these tables, with an estimated 10,000–14,000 permanent exclusions in 1995/96. The Commission for Racial Equality (CRE) described it as, 'the equivalent of dumping the population of a small town each year'.[13] The CRE is right to be concerned — black children make up a disproportionate number of those expelled, and are three times more likely to be excluded than white children.[14]

Exclusions are by no means confined to secondary schools. Indeed, the rate of exclusions is rising more quickly in primary schools than it is in secondary schools. During 1996, for example, there was an 18 per cent increase in exclusions, resulting in 1,400 pupils being expelled from primary schools, accounting for 13 per cent of all school exclusions.[15] Seven per cent of primary schools reported expelling at least one child, and there is even a case of a three-year-old boy being excluded from a pre-school class. More worrying research suggests that primary school children who are permanently excluded lose on average three-quarters of a year's schooling. The average cost of a permanent exclusion is calculated at £4,300 per year.[16]

The figures on truancy — often the first step which leads to exclusion — make equally depressing reading. In 1997, nearly 1 million children, one in eight of the school-age population, missed out on at least one half day's schooling without permission.

Five times as many boys as girls are permanently excluded from school. In secondary schools, 7,191 boys were excluded in 1994/95 compared with 1,663 girls; in primary schools in the same period 1,177

[12] 'Truant pupils blamed for wave of street crime' *The Guardian*, 2 January 1998.

[13] *The Times Educational Supplement,* 15 October 1997.

[14] *The Times Educational Supplement*, 7 November 1997.

[15] *The Times Educational Supplement*, 7 November 1997.

[16] *The Times Educational Supplement*, 10 October 1997.

boys were excluded compared with 91 girls.[17] These figures may
partially explain why more boys than girls commit crime. Leading
educationalist Ted Wragg gave a stark summary of the situation we are
facing as the millennium approaches:

> ... it is the underachievement of boys that has become one of the
> biggest challenges facing society and schools. Improving their
> performance should be given the highest priority by the new
> Government, but not at the expense of girls, whose achievements
> have improved significantly and should continue to do so.[18]

The underachievement of boys can be measured in a variety of ways.
For example, in 1983/84 there was less than a 1 per cent gap in the
number of boys (26.3 per cent) and girls (27.2 per cent) who attained five
high grade GCE passes. By 1995/96 this gap had become a gulf, with
39.8 per cent of boys achieving similar grades at GCSE level, but 49.3
per cent of girls. During the same period there was a similar trend with
A-level results. In 1983/84, 11.1 per cent of boys obtained three or
more A-levels, but only 9.5 per cent of girls. In 1994/95 the figures
were 20.5 per cent for boys, and 24.2 per cent for girls. Not surprisingly
there are now more female undergraduates than male undergraduates
enrolled at universities.

WHAT CAN BE DONE ABOUT YOUTH CRIME?

Our most valuable resource?

For most of the post-war period the approach to young offenders has
been based on principles of welfare rather than punishment; but when
Margaret Thatcher's Government came to power in 1979, her tough
rhetoric on crime was backed up with a promise to give young offenders
a 'short, sharp shock' in custody. However, the population of these
new-style detention centres did not grow at the rate predicted and they
were quietly dropped in the mid-1980s, when evidence of the effects of
their regime suggested that prisoners rather enjoyed the short, sharp
shock. Nevertheless, the Criminal Justice Act 1982 cleared the way for

---

[17] *The Times Educational Supplement*, 16 May 1997.
[18] *ibid.*, All figures quoted are also taken from this article.

more young offenders to be sent to youth custody centres, and between May 1983 and May 1984 the numbers rose by 65 per cent;[19] but youth crime nevertheless continued to rise.

The emphasis of Government policy shifted towards diverting young offenders away from the criminal justice system and keeping them out of custody, and as a consequence the number of juveniles imprisoned in England and Wales fell from 7,900 in 1983 to 2,200 in 1989.[20] This change of emphasis was not as a result of being 'soft' on crime, but rather because there was widespread evidence both of the costs involved in sending young people to custody — it is cheaper to send a boy to Eton than to a young offender institution — and of the ineffectiveness of this approach in helping young people stay out of trouble. (As we demonstrated in Chapter 2, the vast majority of young people who are sent to prison, or young offenders institutions, go on to commit further crime.)

Recorded crime rose sharply in 1990 and 1991 as the economic recession began to take effect, and as a result policy was again reversed. The most obvious examples of this change of direction were the introduction of new secure training orders for 12–14-year-olds, and the establishment of pilot 'boot camps' at HMYOI Thorn Cross and at the Military Corrective Training Centre in Colchester (the latter being abandoned less than a year later). These changes became more urgent with the murder of James Bulger in 1993, and both the Conservatives and New Labour have been prepared to legislate in support of this new direction.

The New Labour approach

The Government's Crime and Disorder Bill promises a 'root and branch' overhaul of the youth justice system. It is likely to centre on three main areas: (i) having the child and his or her parent(s) accept responsibility for wrong-doing; (ii) being 'tough' on youth crime; and (iii) measures designed to attempt to prevent young people committing crime. Specific measures within these three sub-headings include:

---

[19] Eugene McLaughlin and John Muncie (eds), *Controlling Crime*, London: Sage, Open University, 1996.

[20] *ibid.*, p. 267.

- the removal or reform of the common-law presumption of *doli incapax*, which presumes that a child under 14 does not know the difference between right and wrong
- reparation orders, which would require young offenders to make 'reparation' to their victims
- a parenting order, which would require the parents of young offenders to control the criminal behaviour of their children
- a 'final warning' scheme, which will replace police cautions
- an action plan order, which will combine reparation, punishment and rehabilitation to help prevent further crimes being committed
- a supervision order, intended to strengthen existing provision by simplifying breach and enforcement arrangements
- a child safety order, whereby courts will be able to protect children under 10 who are at risk of becoming involved in crime
- local child curfews, which will be imposed by the local authority on children under 10 in a specified public area to help prevent criminal behaviour.

The Bill reflects New Labour's schizophrenic 'tough on crime, tough on the causes of crime' approach. While the emphasis on prevention is welcome, we do not believe that the current approaches being proposed will significantly reduce the amount of youth crime, given that they seem primarily aimed at 'tough' responses when a crime has been committed. More specifically, we are less persuaded that there is a group of 'persistent young offenders' who need to be policed and dealt with accordingly.

Besides the Crime and Disorder Bill, New Labour has also suggested the introduction of 'truancy watch zones', involving local shopkeepers, the local education authority and the police; issuing 'city passes' to schoolchildren who have legitimate reasons to be out of school; and making attendance part of a 'home-school contract' between parents and the school.[21]

This approach may or may not pay dividends, but it is interesting to note that at the heart of these proposals is the desire to shift responsibility from the Government, or indeed the schools, onto parents, and the desire to 'police', regulate, and ultimately punish those who truant, rather than to discover why the child is behaving in this way in the first place.

---

[21] See report in *The Sunday Times*, and *The Sunday Telegraph*, 15 June 1997.

A new approach — prevention is better than cure

We believe that legislation should focus more on preventative measures, which involve investment in our schools so that they are better able to deal with disruptive pupils, and greater support for the parents and families of children at risk. We also believe that there is evidence to suggest that better training and leisure opportunities, especially for older teenagers, will not only deter many from crime, but also help to re-integrate those young people who do commit crime.

Truancy and exclusions

Most of the real solutions to truanting and exclusions involve working more closely with the excluded child, his or her family and teachers to determine together an appropriate plan to re-integrate that pupil back into the classroom. These initiatives do not necessarily involve the injection of significant amounts of money. There are several schools where the approach has proven successful; one of our committee, for example, worked at Bicester Community College where there have been no permanent exclusions in the last 10 years.

The experience of the teachers on our committee, and evidence from a variety of research, suggests that most children truant or become disruptive because they lack the basic literacy and numeracy skills which would allow them to participate in the classroom. This in turn becomes cumulative, so that these children eventually find status and self-esteem not through academic success or employment but through participation in delinquent sub-cultures. Yet experience suggests that adapting the school's curriculum, especially in the last two years of compulsory schooling, in ways which more personally suit the pupil's talents and abilities, will better harness that young person to the culture of the school and to the subsequent needs of living as an adult in the community.

Up and down the country there are examples of good practice in tackling these problems. The North Warwickshire Hard to Place Panel, for instance, was set up to deal with the growing number of excluded children in Warwickshire and to attempt to find them places at other schools so that they could continue with their education. The aim of the scheme, which involves 13 of the county's secondary schools, is to offer such children a second chance. The panel was formed in September

1996, and has made 42 successful placements (from a total of 45) in new schools for children who have been excluded. In effect the heads of the 13 schools working on the panel meet to discuss those pupils who have been excluded, with representatives from social services and the parents and children themselves. The only person not present at the meeting is a representative of the school which excluded the child. A placement is then made to another school. The headmistress of Ash Green School in Exhall, near Coventry, has been able to re-integrate three excluded pupils into her school so far. She recently told *The Times Educational Supplement* about the panel and what it aims to do:

> There is complete trust among the schools taking part. Trust is vital. If the panel decides that I have to take a child, that is fine. I will be told about their history and will try to make sure that the problems do not happen again. I hope (the scheme) will also reduce the risk of these excluded children getting drawn into crime.[22]

Gloucestershire's Education and Social Support Team — known as the ESS — is another innovative example of help being given to children who are in danger of being thrown out of mainstream schooling. Pupils get referred to a member of the team by teachers, social workers and educational psychologists, and are offered classroom support, counselling, or assistance with members of their families to try to deal with the disruptive behaviour so as to keep the child in the classroom. The work of the five-strong ESS team cut the number of school exclusions by 22 between 1993/94 and 1994/95.[23]

As we have seen, there is a growing problem of primary school exclusions. In 1995, Bristol City Council set up a scheme which involves support teachers working together with the school and the child who is in danger of being excluded and his or her parents, as soon as the problem is identified. As such, the support teams not only offer classroom support, but also make available specialist help in the form of referrals to educational psychologists and social workers. As part of the scheme, several schools in the city have also established lunch-time clubs to offer structured activities for pupils who might be disruptive. The results so far have been impressive, and the number of permanent

---

[22] *The Times Educational Supplement*, 24 October 1997.
[23] *The Times Educational Supplement*, 24 October 1997.

exclusions has fallen from 41 in 1994/95 to only 23 in 1996/97. Given the costs of permanent exclusions, the scheme has already paid for the £67,000 grant which was required to set it up.

The Children's Society's Schools Have Inclusive Education — or SHINE — project has also been piloting a scheme which sends two project workers into schools to work with primary school children who are at risk of exclusion. In effect the project workers visit the two London primary schools which have agreed to work with SHINE four mornings a week, to give one-to-one help, or to work with small groups on such issues as friendship and bullying. SHINE also runs parents' groups and advises on the teaching of classroom assistants, in the hope of getting everyone involved with the school to think about how exclusions could be reduced. The project leader commented that the SHINE project shows that

> ... with outside support and the commitment of schools, parents and pupils, children who might otherwise be excluded can be given a real chance. If you are excluded at the age of five, what hope does that give a child for the rest of its life?[24]

An example of SHINE's work in practice comes in the shape of the child, Adrian Thompson, who attends Trinity St Mary's Primary School in Balham, South London. When Adrian was eight his mother, Shirley, was sent a letter by the school advising her that he was in danger of being excluded if his behaviour did not improve. Adrian was hyperactive and kept throwing things across the classroom. He was also being bullied, and as a consequence his reading and writing were suffering. The SHINE project workers identified that part of the problem stemmed from the fact that Mrs Thompson was a nurse who worked shifts, and was therefore not always available when Adrian came home from school. He in turn felt that he had no one to talk to. Arrangements were made so that someone was available for Adrian on his return from school which, allied to one-to-one sessions with his project worker, allowed him to develop his communication skills. Two years later Adrian was still in school and there were significant improvements in his reading, writing, and general commitment to the school.[25]

---

[24] *The Independent*, 23 September 1997.
[25] Adrian's story is told in *The Independent*, above.

We have already drawn attention to the fact that black children, both at primary and secondary schools, are more likely to be excluded than white children. Audrey Osler, a senior lecturer at Birmingham University, directed research into race and school exclusions on behalf of the CRE, and has outlined practical, inexpensive ways of tackling this problem. These include suggestions to:

- ensure that schools which accept excluded pupils are given the money to re-integrate the children successfully
- ensure that sufficient education provision is made by local education authorities for children out of school
- include racial equality as a management issue in headmaster training
- address racial equality issues within training programmes for existing teachers, particularly those which address behaviour management and curriculum leadership
- ensure that equal opportunities issues are central concerns within initial teacher training, alongside numeracy and literacy.

Our committee believes that, in order to address the problem of the disproportionate number of boys who are excluded, the Government should seriously consider adopting the 10-point plan suggested by educationalist Ted Wragg:[26]

- boys should be encouraged to attend nurseries, so that they make an early start on language activities and learn to behave in class
- more fathers should help at home with reading and writing, so that language is not seen as a 'female' activity
- there should be early intervention in school with specialist help offered to boys who cannot read
- more stories should be used which appeal to boys' interests, such as adventure, humour and sport
- more effort should be concentrated on improving boys' behaviour and preventing them from being so easily distracted
- teacher awareness needs to be raised about the underachievement of boys

---

[26] For a fuller account, see T. Wragg, *The Cubic Curriculum*, London: Routledge, 1997. This summary is taken from *The Times Educational Supplement*, 16 May 1997.

- many young boys like using new technology, such as CD Roms, and can often concentrate more when they use it
- more effort needs to be made so as to involve boys in their own learning
- 'at risk' pupils should be identified so that there can be early intervention in primary schools
- there needs to be a coordinated programme for 14- to 18-year-olds in which pupils can choose from a set of what are sometimes called 'academic' and 'vocational' modules, so that programmes can be tailored to individual needs and interests.

Breaking the cycle of offending

It is our belief that we need to adopt a different approach to young people who commit crime, which acknowledges the realities of the crimes which they commit and the evidence which exists as to what will deter them from committing criminal acts. This is neither too soft nor too tough, but merely reflects what is happening in our country to our young people. As such, we propose to stand back from the soundbite approach to policy, and instead to look for more rational and effective solutions. In doing so we would like to promote a virtuous circle which would see less crime, less spending on crime, and more spending on crime prevention.

Up and down the country there are many examples of a variety of groups and agencies, working with young people in positive ways to divert them from crime. Perhaps the best known is the 'Dalston Youth Project'.[27] The project was established in 1994 to work with some of the most alienated young people living in Hackney. The London borough has very high risk factors associated with offending, such as high rates of school exclusions, unemployment and truancy, and in 1993 it had the highest recorded crime levels in the whole of London. Police, probation and social workers, teachers or simply members of the community can refer young people aged between 15 and 19 to the project, on the basis of that young person's exclusion from school or involvement in crime. The project involves pairing the young person with a mentor, who is a volunteer recruited from the local community. Groups of mentors and

---

[27] See the report of Y. Burgin, 'The Panacea: The Evidence in Favour of the Dalston Youth Project' in *Criminal Justice Matters*, No. 28, Summer 1997.

young people meet for a week-long, intensive residential course, where the young person is helped to look at his or her life, and thereafter work together on a weekly basis. There is also a two-month 'college taster' at Hackney Community College, which provides literacy and numeracy tuition. Lastly, the project organises a series of work placements, which in 1996 included work experience at Kiss FM, the *Daily Mirror*, and Choice FM. As yet there has been no academic evaluation of the Dalston Youth Project, but at the end of the first year's intake over half had gone on to full-time education, work or training.

Similarly, 'Drive for Youth' is dedicated to giving young unemployed people the skills and confidence to find work. Each year it runs nine 22-week courses of personal development and employment-based training for disaffected young people between the ages of 18 and 24. Groups of young people spend five weeks at the charity's training centre in Snowdonia, where they work in teams to explore strengths and weaknesses through discussion and outdoor pursuits. In doing so they are encouraged to learn a sense of personal responsibility and leadership skills. Paul Williams, who enrolled on a 'Drive for Youth' course in the autumn of 1996, described its effect on him:

> I was a bit of a naughty lad when I was younger. I had several minor skirmishes with the Law ... I got myself stuck in a bad rut ... my quality of life was appalling really. I did not seem to have time for anything before DFY — I looked after number one ... [DFY] opened my eyes and made me consider other people's feelings and needs ... If you are willing to learn what it does is amazing.[28]

A more direct example of a scheme dealing with young offenders is the 'Milton Keynes Retail Theft Initiative', which was reported on by the Home Office in 1997. It is aimed at young shoplifters to educate them to appreciate that shoplifting is not a victimless crime; to understand the consequences of their actions; and to prevent future offending. A formal police caution is given on completion of the scheme. Attendance is voluntary, and Home Office research has shown that there was a re-offending rate of 3 per cent during the period of the

---

[28] Quoted in *The Times Educational Supplement*, 17 October 1997.

study, compared with a rate of 35 per cent for first-time offenders dealt with in other ways.[29]

Several other schemes of this kind exist, usually partly-run or sponsored by the probation service, but our final example relates to the 'Salford Community Link Project', which was initially sponsored by NACRO. This has received widespread attention, as it was for this project that Eric Cantona was required to run coaching sessions as part of his 120 hours' community service order. What received less attention was the effect that the project had on young people in Salford before Cantona arrived, and after he had left.

The project was launched in 1994, and was aimed at young people between 8 and 16 who otherwise lacked leisure opportunities. Its aim was to divert young people away from anti-social behaviour and instead to encourage positive relationships to develop between the adults involved with the project and young people. Despite being initiated by NACRO, once established, the project has been run by over 100 local volunteers, in 18 clubs, involving 980 participants. The adult volunteers organise training sessions, matches, tournaments, league competitions and social events. As such the project has attracted youngsters from a variety of backgrounds, including those who are at risk of, or have been convicted of, crime, or who have significant behavioural problems. The project costs £1.80 per week per participant.

A study of the last three years of the project[30] shows that participants have improved their self-confidence and channelled their energies away from causing trouble. The relationships that have developed between the young people and the adult volunteers have also played an important role, and have therefore also been of value to the volunteers. Indeed, many of the adult volunteers have also experienced long-term unemployment and been in trouble with the law. Commenting on the scheme, Jim Smith, Community Affairs Inspector for the Greater Manchester Police, said: 'I have seen dramatic effects resulting from the setting up of football teams in some areas. Young people connected in activities such as these are far less likely to get involved in crime and disorder.'

---

[29] Research quoted in Lord Bingham of Cornhill, *Justice for the Young*, London: PRT, 1997, p. 9.

[30] NACRO, *City United: The First Three Years of the Salford Community Link Project*, London: NACRO, 1997. All quotes used are taken from this document.

The benefits to the local community have also been immense. Dave Eglin, for example, from the Brookhouse Estate Residents' Association, described the difference to the estate when their club started:

> The Brookhouse Estate has 1,000 homes and 46 per cent unemployment. There's a huge population of kids with absolutely nothing for them to do on the estate. They were out kicking balls around, breaking windows at the school and causing havoc at the shops. It's got a bad reputation the Brookhouse, which isn't fair as it's alright really. When the youth club first re-opened only 3 people came ... now we've 40 or so kids — they're the ones who'd be out on the streets otherwise.

Similarly, one community worker noted that

> ... we use the football project as a base, bringing lots of different people together. Rival gangs congregate in the same area for the same aims and there's no trouble — they've formed bonds with other kids and adults ... we're taking them off the street corners and keeping them off.

All of this seems a far more positive way of dealing with young people than curfews and school exclusions. Given that some 3 million people in this country play football on a regular basis, just think about what the Salford scheme applied across the whole country might achieve.

The Scottish system

Lastly, we would like to draw attention to the Scottish system of youth justice. Following the Kilbrandon Report of 1964, Scotland dismantled its juvenile courts and created in their place a new system based on panel hearings. Scotland took this decision because it was believed that a court could not act both as a criminal court and as a treatment agency. As such, decisions are made solely to promote the welfare of the child. In terms of disposal of a young offender, the most obvious difference between the Scottish and the English and Welsh systems is that in Scotland there is no penal custody available to the children's hearing for those under 16, reflecting the belief that such a sentence would be incompatible with the welfare needs of the child.

The most important figure in the Scottish system is the Reporter, a qualified lawyer, to whom information is passed by a variety of agencies about the child in difficulty. Children under 16 can be referred to the Reporter for a variety of reasons, including failure to attend school, lack of parental care, or being 'out of control'. Similarly, young offenders appearing in the Sheriff Court between the ages of 16 and 18 can also be referred to the children's hearing. In effect the Reporter looks into the case of the child to decide what action, if any, needs to be taken.

The proceedings of children's hearings are informal and the parents of the child are required to attend, as is the child. The hearing is presided over by a panel of three, who have very extensive powers. They can, for example, simply discuss the case, or they can impose a supervision requirement for a year, renewable until the child is 18. In most cases a supervised child remains at home, under the supervision of a social worker.

Think about how the application of the Scottish system might impact on our disposal of young people in England and Wales. Our nearest neighbour isn't experimenting with boot camps and secure treatment centres, but has instead steadfastly dealt with difficult juveniles in a far more humane way.

CONCLUSION

We have spent some considerable time describing the experiences of young people, both at school and as offenders, and we make no apology for doing so. We believe that if our country is to prosper we need to value and understand our young people, and to invest in them with our time and efforts. Yet, for a variety of reasons, too many sectors of our society do not view young people in that way, but rather as a group which has to be feared, policed and controlled. This fear has in turn resulted in a variety of 'tough' proposals being considered and introduced against the interests of young people. As we hope we have demonstrated, we do not believe that these are necessary; nor is there much evidence to suggest that they will prove to be effective. We urge everyone who cares about the future of our country to re-think radically how we respond to our young people, and to assess the evidence of 'what works' with those few young people who commit crime.

5 Race and Criminal Justice

What percentage of the British population is made up of people from ethnic minorities? This is a fairly straightforward question, but one which rarely gets answered correctly. At a recent lecture given by one of the authors to over 100 first-year undergraduates in criminal justice, many of whom were black or Asian, the most common answer was 35 per cent. This is not unusual as a reply, whether the question is being asked of students, magistrates, police officers or (we imagine) readers of this book. So, what percentage of the British population *is* made up of people from ethnic minorities? The answer is 5.5 per cent.

Clearly if you lived in Brixton or Handsworth this figure would be higher, but as an average, across the whole country, the British population is 94.5 per cent white and only 5.5 per cent black.[1] Why do so many people believe that the figure is much higher?

Obviously our perception of what is happening around us is shaped by several factors. Personal experience, what politicians tell us, what we see on our televisions, or read in our newspapers, all contribute to our understanding of race in this country. As such, many might be persuaded that Britain is being 'swamped' by black people — most of whom would fail the loyalty 'cricket test' to Britain if the people being described are Afro-Caribbean, or who may be deemed to be 'fundamentalist' and terrorists if they are Muslims. (Indeed, so great has the fear of Muslim

---

[1] We are using the term 'black' to include all Afro-Caribbean and Asian groups and sub-groups, despite the many differences, as opposed to similarities between these groups. We will draw attention to these differences where appropriate.

people become that a new word — Islamophobia — has had to be invented to describe our anxiety.)

This fear of 'Islam' is indicative of other, more general fears concerning black people — in particular that they are more likely to commit crime than white people. This is most often seen in our fear of black youths, who frequently are stereotyped as predators who have made our streets unsafe. In July 1995, for example, Sir Paul Condon, the Metropolitan Police Commissioner, urged ethnic community leaders to recognise that 'it is a fact that very many of the perpetrators of muggings are very young black people'.[2] His comments caused uproar, especially as many of the victims of these muggings were themselves young black people; nor did he draw attention to racial attacks on young black people by white youths. One might also question his tactics, given that Sir Paul's comments were aimed at urging ethnic minority community leaders to join with him in a new initiative to combat street crime.

In one sense Sir Paul's remarks were taken out of context, and it is a pity that not everything which he said was reported in full. For example, the widely reported statement that 'it is a fact that very many of the perpetrators of muggings are very young black people', is only half of a sentence which ends 'who have been excluded from school and/or are unemployed'. This makes a quite different point from the one which emerged in the media.

In any event, his comments merely confirmed the already widespread distrust between the various black communities and the criminal justice system, which has existed for some time. After all, a variety of evidence exists to suggest that black people are over-represented as clients of the criminal justice system but under-represented as members of its staff. Research exists to show that at every stage of the policing, sentencing, imprisonment or probationary process, discrimination against black people takes place; despite the fact that research also shows that black people are more likely to be the victims, rather than the perpetrators, of crime. This knowledge led one former Conservative Home Office Minister to conclude in 1991 that

> I [am] a reluctant convert to the view that there appears to be an element of discrimination against ethnic minority offenders in our

---

[2] These comments received wide press coverage. See *The Daily Telegraph*, 7 July 1996.

criminal processes ... The fabric of our society is only sustainable if the mass of society consents to the criteria on which justice is administered. If a particular discrete, identifiable and self-identifiable sector of that society believe that there is a system of justice which is just for other people, but not just for them, whether or not that belief is well founded, the effects upon our society as a whole will be very damaging because those people will see the judicial system not as a means for maintaining law and order but as a means for keeping 'them' down and 'us' up. That is a recipe for internecine warfare and is very dangerous.[3]

This chapter examines the experiences of black people in the criminal justice system, and ends with some conclusions as to what we need to do so as to ensure that justice for all rather than 'internecine warfare' is encouraged and promoted in our community.

ARE BLACK PEOPLE MORE LIKELY THAN WHITE PEOPLE TO COMMIT CRIME?

One of our colleagues is a British-born Jamaican man in his early '30s. Recently he was travelling from London to Rugby where he was to deliver one of the annual Perrie Lectures — a cross-criminal justice forum which has attracted Tony Blair as a speaker. He described walking along the platform at Euston, dressed in an Armani suit, white shirt with a button-down collar, silk tie, and highly polished shoes. In short, the perfect picture of success and conservatism. Some other passengers didn't see him as such and, as he passed, three elderly white women each moved their handbags out of view. This everyday scene of distrust and suspicion from the drama which is the British view of ethnic minorities and crime, is almost so common that black people rarely comment upon it. Our colleague chose to do so because the three elderly ladies turned up at his lecture.

Are black people more likely to commit crime than white people? The most recent Home Office research, published in 1995, analysed self-reported crimes admitted in confidential interviews of a random

---

[3] Lord Elton, quoted in Penal Affairs Consortium, *Race and Criminal Justice*, London: NACRO, 1996, p. 2.

sample of 1,721 young people between the ages of 14 and 25, with a booster sample of 808 young people of the same age from ethnic minority groups. This age group is significant, as it is people in this age range who are the perpetrators of most of the crimes which dominate our recorded criminal statistics, and a higher proportion of the black than white population are in this age group. Nonetheless, young Afro-Caribbeans and whites had similar rates of offending, while young Asian people had lower rates. Indeed, contrary to popular stereotypes, white youngsters also indicated that they were more likely to use illegal drugs than Afro-Caribbeans, and Asians were less likely to do so than either group. Perhaps this stereotype is beginning to change anyway, with the revelation that the Home Secretary's 17-year-old son is alleged to have dealt in cannabis.

Another way of looking at this question is to consider who is more likely to be the victim of crime, and this is also best done through confidential and self-report surveys. The 1988 BCS for the first time used a booster sample of just over 700 Afro-Caribbeans and nearly 1,000 Asian people to consider whether they were disproportionately likely to be victims of crime, and the extent to which there was a racial element in the offences which they experienced. The research concluded that both Afro-Caribbeans and Asians were 'more likely to become victims of crime than whites':[4]

> Afro-Caribbeans are more likely to experience burglary (especially where there is a successful entry into their houses). Those who own cars and bikes are more prone to thefts than whites, and many of these thefts take place near to home. Afro-Caribbeans are more likely to be assaulted, threatened and to suffer robbery or theft from the person.[5]

These findings go some way to explaining the uproar which greeted the remarks of Sir Paul Condon, and to providing some balance to a stereotypical portrayal of who commits crime in this country. However, it should also be remembered that most of the crime which is recorded — and that which is reported in victim surveys — tends to be concentrated in areas of high unemployment, with poorer housing inhabited by younger households. Black people are over-represented in

---

[4] The 1988 British Crime Survey, London: HMSO, 1989, p. 47.
[5] *ibid.*, p. 42.

this type of area which is more 'prone' to crime, which thus merely re-inforces the law-abiding nature of the black community.

BLACK PEOPLE AND THE CRIMINAL JUSTICE SYSTEM: PRISON

There are opportunities to exercise discretion at every stage of the criminal justice process: from the decision of a police officer to stop and search an individual, and whether or not that person is cautioned, to decisions taken about that individual in relation to whether or not he or she should be remanded in custody or bailed; whether he or she should be given a community-based penalty, or a sentence of custody; and lastly, discretion in relation to how long that period of imprisonment should be. Our belief, which is supported by research, is that discretion provides opportunities for discrimination, and that the impact of that discrimination becomes cumulative. This is particularly true in circumstances where discretion can be exercised:

- without clear guidelines setting out specific criteria
- where decisions are based on subjective judgement
- where there is no requirement to record and monitor the reasons for a decision being taken, and
- where decision-making is influenced by organisational 'cultures' rather than by objective variations in circumstances, or by the requirements of service delivery.

All of this has led several commentators to conclude that different decisions are taken about different groups at key stages of the criminal justice process, and that ethnic minorities and whites have very different patterns of contact within the criminal justice system. This conclusion is most obvious in relation to imprisonment.[6]

The prison population of England and Wales contains a disproportionally high number of black prisoners. In 1995, 17 per cent of all male prisoners and 24 per cent of female prisoners were black. Afro-Caribbeans are particularly over-represented; despite their accounting for only 1.5 per cent of the general population, Afro-Caribbeans make

---

[6] See M. Fitzgerald, *Ethnic Minorities and the Criminal Justice System*, London: HMSO, 1993, which summarises the research of several studies.

up 11 per cent and 20 per cent of the male and female prison populations respectively.[7] Three per cent of all prisoners were of Indian, Pakistani or Bangladeshi origin in 1995, in comparison with 2.7 per cent of the general population.

Many of the Indian, Pakistani and Bangladeshi prisoners are Muslims, and some recent research has shown how Muslims are discriminated against while in prison.[8] Despite HM Prison Service's race relations policy statement, Muslims faced difficulties in maintaining their religion, especially during Ramadan. One prisoner described his experiences in the following way:

> As you know it is Ramadan for Muslims in here. Many of us have been forced to come off the fast as the organisation and food have been terrible. No one consulted us in trying to work out the arrangements. It has deeply hurt me.[9]

The problems faced by Muslim prisoners are only beginning to be researched and understood. However, the prison experiences of Afro-Caribbean prisoners have long been a focus of study for penologists.[10] These studies have shown that Afro-Caribbeans are often discriminated against in allocations to work, transfer arrangements and access to education facilities, and are disproportionately placed on charges for offences against prison discipline. It should be remembered that this discrimination takes place despite the prison service's own policy statements regarding race in prisons.

The tragic death of Alton Manning, a black prisoner remanded in custody at UK Detention Services Limited's HMP Blakenhurst, in December 1995 from positional asphyxia can be viewed as a dramatic example of the realities of institutional racism in our prisons. The jury in the inquest into the death of Mr Manning, which was conducted in March 1998, decided that he had been 'unlawfully killed' by the eight prison officers who had restrained him. Further controversy was caused

---

[7] Penal Affairs Consortium, *Race and Criminal Justice*, , London: NACRO, 1996, p. 2.

[8] D. Wilson and D. Sharp, *Visiting Prisons: A Handbook for Imams*, London: IQRA Trust, 1998.

[9] Quoted in K. McDermott, We Have No Problems: The Experience of Racism in Prison, *New Community*, 16(2), pp. 213-228.

[10] See in particular E. Genders and E. Player, *Race Relations in Prisons*, Oxford: Clarendon Press, 1989.

when, on being interviewed on the BBC's *Newsnight*, Richard Tilt, the Director General of the prison service, suggested that the reason why six of the seven prisoners who had died in prison in this very way had been black, was as a result that 'Afro-Caribbean people are more likely to suffer positional asphyxia than whites'. This assertion is not based on fact and Mr Tilt was forced to apologise for his remarks.

It might be tempting to view the numbers of black people in prison as proof that they commit more crime. However, successive analyses of prison statistics have shown that black people who commit offences are more likely to end up in prison than comparable white offenders, and that black people entering prison have on average fewer previous convictions than white people.[11] This would seem to confirm that there is discrimination in the criminal justice process at those stages prior to imprisonment.

BLACK PEOPLE AND THE CRIMINAL JUSTICE SYSTEM: POLICING AND STAFFING

A barrage of research confirms that there are very different patterns of contact with the police for ethnic minorities than for whites. For example, in March 1996 the Home Office published figures detailing the number of people stopped and searched by the police in 1994/95, broken down by police force area and ethnic group. In England and Wales a total of 590,918 people were stopped and searched, of whom 131,579 (22 per cent) were from ethnic minority groups. The Metropolitan Police stopped and searched 112,763 people from ethnic minority groups out of a total of 302,691, which represents 37 per cent of those stopped and searched, the highest proportion of any police force area.[12] It is also interesting to remember that these figures are taken from the same year that Sir Paul Condon made his remarks about young black people and muggings (see above). This pattern of stop and search would seem to have existed for some time. Research from the mid-1980s by the Policy Studies Institute showed that of all the people stopped and searched by the Metropolitan Police, 63 per cent were Afro-Caribbean, 44 per cent were white, and 18 per cent were Asian.

---

[11] *ibid.*

[12] *ibid.* Figure quoted on p. 6.

Interestingly, only a very small proportion of those who are stopped and searched are in fact arrested, but again there is a wide variation in the experiences of different people once arrested, based on their ethnic group. Young Afro-Caribbeans, for example, are less likely than young white people to be cautioned, although there is some evidence to suggest that this is as a result of a higher proportion of young Afro-Caribbeans denying the charge, which would prevent a caution being given. Nonetheless, in 1992 the CRE in an academic study concerning decisions to caution or prosecute young people in several police force areas, found that

in the majority of forces, proportionally more ethnic minority young people — and particularly Afro-Caribbeans — were referred for prosecution than white young people; in inner-city areas the difference was very substantial indeed. The widespread police view that such differences would indicate that, on average, ethnic minority young people were committing more serious offences was not borne out. Statistical controls for 'offence type' (such as burglary, robbery etc.) suggested that this factor played a very small part in explaining the differences in prosecution rates. Controls for the number of past offences also suggested that this was not the main explanation.[13]

Similarly, the overall pattern of charges brought against Afro-Caribbeans differs from that of whites or Asians, and several researchers have commented upon the fact that Afro-Caribbeans are more likely to be charged with indictable offences only, which means that their cases will be heard in the Crown Court. There is also evidence to suggest that Afro-Caribbeans are more likely to be remanded in custody than given bail.[14]

In relation to sentencing at Crown Court, the most thorough research has been that conducted by Dr Roger Hood, Director of the Centre for Criminological Research at Oxford University, which was published in 1992.[15] Hood examined the sentences passed in 3,317 cases heard by the Crown Courts at Dudley, Coventry, Birmingham, Warwick and Stafford

---

[13] Commission for Racial Equality, *Cautions and Prosecutions*, London: Commission for Racial Equality, 1992.

[14] See, for example, *Race and Criminal Justice*, London: HMSO, 1992, p. 3.

[15] R. Hood, *Race and Sentencing: A Study in the Crown Court*, Oxford: Clarendon Press, 1992. All figures are taken from this work.

during 1989. Overall, black males were 17 per cent more likely to receive a custodial sentence than white males. Even after taking into account 15 key variables relating to the seriousness of the offence and other factors, Hood found that black people had a 5–8 per cent greater overall chance of going to prison. In cases of medium gravity, where judges had much greater discretion than in the most serious cases, the difference was 13 per cent. The study also found that significantly higher proportions of black (42 per cent) and Asian (43 per cent) offenders were sentenced without a social inquiry report being available to the court, compared with 28 per cent of white offenders. Social inquiry reports are a very obvious way to mitigate on behalf of the offender, explaining his or her personal domestic circumstances and how these might have affected the offending behaviour. Their absence is therefore likely to contribute to that offender going to prison, and for longer periods of time.

Hood also discovered that there were significant differences between the courts examined. In Dudley, for example, black offenders had a 23 per cent higher chance of receiving a custodial sentence than white offenders, when the key variables had been allowed for; at Warwick and Stafford, black people were also considerably more likely to receive a prison sentence. Thankfully this did not occur in the case of Davinder and Lakhbir Deol, who found themselves in Stafford Crown Court in 1994 as a result of being charged with the murder of a man who had repeatedly made racist attacks on the Deols and their business in Stoke-on-Trent, eventually driving them out of town.[16] Perhaps we can account for their acquittal given the awful evidence of racism at the heart of the case. Having survived the riots in Handsworth in 1985, the Deols outlined a catalogue of vicious racism directed against them, including taunts, intimidation, physical assault, and the routine criminal destruction of their business, including by fire-bombings.

Hood found no difference between the various ethnic groups and the likelihood of custody at Birmingham Crown Court, but he again found significant racial disparities in the distribution of non-custodial sentences at the various courts. After taking account of the factors influencing the severity of the sentence, it was found that black adults were given higher tariff sentences than whites, especially those sentenced at

---

[16] An account of the Deols' ordeal can be found in D. Rose, *In the Name of the Law: The Collapse of Criminal Justice*, London: Vintage, 1996, pp. 51–66.

Dudley. Black offenders were more likely than whites, for example, to receive a suspended prison sentence; less likely to be given a community service or a probation order; less likely to be recommended for probation; and, even when recommended for probation, less likely to get it than white offenders.

In conclusion the study estimated that:

> 80 per cent of the over-representation of black men in the prison population was due to the disproportionate number of them appearing in the Crown Courts (reflecting, of course, decisions made at all previous stages of the criminal justice process) and the seriousness of their cases. The remaining 20 per cent ... could only be explained as a result of the differential treatment by the courts and other factors influencing the use of custody and the severity of the sentences they received. One third of this 'race effect' was due to the higher proportion pleading not guilty with the larger prison terms they got as a result ... it would not need very many courts to behave as the Dudley courts and the courts of Warwick or Stafford appear to have done for it to have a considerable disproportionate effect on the racial composition of the prison population.[17]

In short, to return to where we started, the disproportionate numbers of ethnic minorities imprisoned stem from profound, consistent and cumulative discrimination at every stage of our criminal justice system, and Afro-Caribbeans are most likely to suffer from that discrimination.

BLACK PEOPLE AS STAFF WITHIN THE CRIMINAL JUSTICE SYSTEM

People from ethnic minorities might be over-represented amongst those on the 'receiving end' of the criminal justice system, but they are significantly under-represented as members of its staff. This is important, for if black people are to feel that (in the words of Lord Elton) the criminal justice system represents 'them' as opposed to simply keeping them down, and that it promotes justice for everyone, no matter the colour of their skin, then the number and seniority of black people

---

[17] *ibid.,* Hood (1992)

working within the criminal justice system is of relevance. Yet a report in 1996, reflecting figures from 1995, by the National Association of Probation Offices and the Association of Black Probation Officers, found under-representation of black people as staff in almost every agency associated with the criminal justice system. A brief survey of these agencies demonstrates the extent of the problem:

- there are no High Court judges from ethnic minority groups. In 1995, only five of the 514 circuit judges, two of the 339 district judges, 13 of the 897 recorders, and nine of the 314 assistant recorders were from ethnic minority groups
- eight point one per cent of newly appointed magistrates in 1995 were from ethnic minorities, but there were no black justices' clerks, and only 17 of 370 deputy clerks, and 21 of the 1,470 court ushers were from ethnic minority groups
- prior to training being provided by NACRO's race unit, only four of the 248 Crown Prosecution Service's staff in grades 1 to 6 (1.6 per cent) and 90 of the Service's 1,255 legal assistants (7.1 per cent) were from ethnic minority groups
- in September 1995, 2,223 (1.75 per cent) of the 127,222 police officers were from ethnic minority groups; 36 Inspectors, 8 Chief Inspectors, and 1 Superintendent had ethnic minority backgrounds
- figures from the same year reveal that only five of HM Prison Service's 1,020 governor grades (0.49 per cent) and 354 out of 19,325 prison officers (2.4 per cent) were from ethnic minority groups
- five hundred and eighty-five of the 7,905 probation officers (7.6 per cent) were from ethnic minority groups, compared with 2.6 per cent in 1989. The number of senior probation officers from ethnic minority groups has risen during this period from three to 42 in 1995 (from 0.26 per cent to 3.4 per cent). As yet there are no black chief probation officers, but reflecting the probation service's positive record in this matter, eight members of ethnic minority groups were in senior management positions
- in June 1995, 4 per cent of solicitors and 6 per cent of barristers were from ethnic minority groups, representing significant improvements since 1989.[18]

---

[18] All figures are quoted in Penal Affairs Consortium (1996), pp. 6–7.

These last figures do represent an increase in the numbers of black lawyers; and indeed, since 1995 many of the agencies described would be able in some way or another to mount some defence in relation to their recruitment policies. However, this does not go far enough. Lincoln Crawford, for example, Chairman of the Bar Race Relations Committee, despite the increase in the numbers of black solicitors and barristers, was still able to describe in 1997 a 'concrete ceiling' against ethnic minority lawyers. Indeed, he described a conversation with one chambers clerk who commented that 'we are comfortable now with Asian barristers, but as far as Afro-Caribbean ones — we're just not ready for them, the clients wouldn't like it'.[19] Crawford went on to outline the obstacles faced by ethnic minority lawyers at every stage of their legal career, from acceptance to law school and professional examinations, to entry into a law firm or chambers, and finally when it comes to promotion to the bench. He concluded that 'You can't talk about a multicultural society where there are whole swath's of areas in the legal profession where black people cannot participate at all.'[20]

It is our belief that Crawford's comments would also serve as an accurate reflection of the current experiences of people from ethnic minorities in the police, probation service and prison service. Robin Alfred's research on black workers in the prison service, for example, largely conducted through personal interviews with several black staff working in the prison service concluded that there is 'a wide gap between management formulated policy and the attitude and practices of uniformed prison officers'.[21] He describes the personal and institutional racism faced by black staff within prisons, making them reluctant to accept promotion where the pressures would be greater. He quotes one black officer describing white staff 'calling inmates "niggers", "coon" ... you think that's gone out of the window? Well, it hasn't';[22] and tells of black applicants being asked different questions than white applicants during selection interviews. Similarly, he quotes other research describing the open flaunting of racist badges and insignia worn by some staff, and one civilian instructor who wouldn't have black prisoners employed in his workshop. The instructor's rationale was 'you

---

[19] *The Times*, 18 November 1997.
[20] *ibid.*
[21] R. Alfred, *Black Workers in the Prison Service*, London: Prison Reform Trust, 1992, p. iv.
[22] *ibid.*, p. 27.

just can't have them doing this job. It would be different, wouldn't it, if it was a banana factory I was running here — then it would be right up their street'.[23]

HOPE FOR A MORE JUST FUTURE FOR BLACK PEOPLE

Section 95 of the Criminal Justice Act 1991 requires the Home Secretary to publish on an annual basis information which helps people engaged in the administration of justice to avoid discrimination. This is important as it not only requires information about race and criminal justice to be published — which has led to a variety of monitoring initiatives — but it is also the first explicit recognition in statute law of the existence of a duty to avoid discrimination in the administration of justice. The aim of the monitoring undertaken by the various criminal justice agencies is to put in place a system that will be able to track a defendant's progress through the criminal justice system. Thus:

- in 1996 all police force areas were required to monitor arrests, cautions, stop and search, and homicide ethnically
- the Crown Prosecution Service (CPS) has drawn up a sample monitoring scheme for the year 1996–97 involving the random sampling of 4,000 cases. The exercise will involve the monitoring of bail and recommendations; charge alterations for a number of specific offences; mode of trial recommendations; and discontinuance
- a national system for race and ethnic monitoring was introduced into the probation service in 1992, and in the same year the prison service introduced new ethnic monitoring codes to ensure consistency with other agencies.

However, monitoring goes only so far in improving this sorry tale of discrimination described above. Hand in glove with monitoring there need to be changes in the policy and practice of criminal justice. Indeed, there have been some good examples of change which, if given the right support, would contribute greatly to avoiding discrimination. For example, the Law Society and the Bar have established Race Relations

---

[23] *ibid.*, pp. 26–27.

Committees, and the Association of Chief Police Officers and the Commission for Racial Equality have issued a practical guide to all police force areas entitled *Policing and Racial Equality*. Similarly, the CPS and the prison service have adopted policy statements on race relations, and in 1993 the Home Office provided funding for NACRO's Race Unit to work at a local level to help criminal justice agencies translate these policy statements into action. Further funding has since been provided so that the Race Unit can work with the 23 Area Criminal Justice Liaison Committees to ensure that race issues are a very visible part of their agendas.

Yet no matter how good these initiatives are, and how valuable they might become, the continuing everyday experiences of black people who encounter the criminal justice system remain overwhelmingly negative, and there is a long way yet to travel. The case of Stephen Lawrence is the most high-profile indication of this conclusion, but we will use less well-known and anecdotal examples to illustrate this point further. In doing so we hope to demonstrate that practical realities are often very different from policy and 'mission statements', proudly displayed on office walls and on the exteriors of buildings. Similarly, we detect a sense that re-opening the case of Stephen Lawrence will merely serve to suggest to many that there really is not too much to worry about and that resolving this matter will put things 'right'. However, our evidence and the experience of our committee suggests that, although discrimination may be increasingly less high-profile, it is woven into the often hidden fabric of our organisations and their cultures.

One of our committee was a member of a three-person panel interviewing candidates for the post of senior officer in HM Prison Service. As such, he asked each candidate whether racial jokes had any part to play in promoting good race relations, in the hope that this would allow the candidates to describe HM Prison Service's race relations policy statement described above. Very few candidates were able to deal satisfactorily with this question, but one replied that racial jokes were good 'ice breakers' and then proceeded to tell a racial joke. The same governor was also assured that his privatised catering company was supplying halal meat to Muslim prisoners within the jail. This proved to be a lie, which was uncovered only when the governor demanded (during Ramadan) to see the receipts from the Halal butcher.

These anecdotes demonstrate that a comprehensive programme of action needs to be undertaken so as to ensure that policy statements, and the work of race relations committees, are translated into action. Based on the evidence available to our committee, we would suggest that:

- training in race relations matters should be provided to decision-makers within criminal justice agencies. Too often race relations training is seen as something which is necessary merely for those at the lower levels of command, rather than for those who exercise power and discretion
- greater efforts should be made in all criminal justice agencies to recruit and retain staff from ethnic minorities. This might mean that we need to consider such issues as positive discrimination so as to ensure that we have suitable numbers of staff from these groups working within criminal justice agencies. This positive discrimination might take a variety of forms, such as all-black promotion lists, but need not continue indefinitely
- the growing evidence from the racial monitoring which is being undertaken is analysed, published and that the results of this analysis is fed back into the decision-making process, so that areas of discrimination can be eradicated.

In doing all of this we hope it will be possible to achieve a criminal justice system which is free from racial discrimination and just for all sections of our community, irrespective of their colour or ethnic origin.

6   Women and the Criminal Justice System

WOMEN OFFENDERS

Late in September 1997, Peter Fisher made a special journey from his home in Warley, West Midlands, to visit the Royal Academy's new exhibition of young British artists from the Saatchi collection. The exhibition was called *Sensation*, and included work by Damien Hirst, Fiona Rae, and Gillian Wearing. However, Peter Fisher was no art lover. On entering the gallery he made immediately for Marcus Harvey's re-working of Myra Hindley's police photograph, taken in 1966, and covered it in Indian ink. As Fisher, a father of two explained: 'I did it on behalf of parents everywhere. I am glad I did it, and I only wish that I had time to destroy it.'

Overwhelmingly it is men who come to the attention of the police, the courts and the probation service, and who end up in prison. Yet, despite — or perhaps because of — this relationship between masculinity and offending, the small number of women who commit crimes — especially crimes of a violent or sexual nature — arouse the greatest controversy. Our society seems to have higher expectations of a woman's behaviour than of a man's. Characteristics such as assertiveness, aggression or independence, all of which would be seen as highly desirable in a man, are regarded as suspect in a woman.

Undoubtedly the crimes of Myra Hindley, Rosemary West, Tracie Andrews and female murderers are all the more shocking because the perpetrators are women. No matter what their personal background or circumstances, women are somehow expected to be instinctive wives and mothers, and also passive and submissive in their temperament. Thus any woman who commits a violent or sexual crime, especially against a child, is automatically seen to have broken an idealised feminine 'type', and correspondingly forfeits society's respect. It is likely that Peter Fisher was merely doing something that many others would have liked to have done themselves, and not just to Hindley's portrait. Indeed, just months after the attack on the picture, the Home Secretary decided that Hindley, who has been in custody for 31 years, would spend the rest of her life in prison, with no prospect of parole.

Horrific crimes such as the 'Moors Murders' are extremely rare, and the problems posed by what to do with a woman who offends in this way — albeit in the company of a more dominant, male accomplice — are a distraction from the reality of offending by women in this country. Only a relatively small number of women are in prison for violence: in 1996, around 20 per cent of women offenders were in custody for offences, or alleged offences, of violence against the person; and most female offenders were incarcerated for minor property offences.[1] Typically these minor property offences include theft, shoplifting, fraud, benefit fraud, and using stolen cheque books and credit cards, often to feed a drug habit.

Similarly, female prisoners tend to have less serious criminal records than their male counterparts, both in terms of previous convictions and in terms of the gravity of those offences. For example, a survey in 1993/94 of women entering HMP Holloway, the largest women's prison in Western Europe, showed that two-thirds of the prisoners held had never been in prison before. (This finding has been confirmed by a recent thematic review of women's imprisonment by HM Chief Inspector of Prisons, which discovered that 71 per cent of women in custody during 1996 had never previously had a custodial sentence.)[2] Some of these women had been imprisoned for very minor offences indeed. Astonishingly, just under 40 per cent of all women prosecuted for offences in this country are charged with not having a licence for their television, and every week five or six women come into HMP

---

[1] Prison Reform Trust, *Women in Prison: Recent Trends and Developments*, London: PRT, 1996, p. 1.

[2] HM Chief Inspector of Prisons, *Women in Prison: A Thematic Review*, London: Home Office, 1997, p. 13.

Holloway for non-payment of a TV licence. Indeed at any given time, 5 per cent of the population of the prison are fine defaulters.[3]

Other characteristics of the female prison population, confirmed by a variety of research conducted over a period of time, would suggest that:

- most women imprisoned have never been in prison before
- women from ethnic minorities are disproportionately represented in the prison population
- most female prisoners have poor employment and educational histories
- they have accommodation problems
- significant numbers have suffered physical and sexual abuse
- they are serious drug misusers, and
- many are mothers of children under the age of 16.

This last characteristic is of great concern. The Prison Reform Trust found that 70 per cent of HMP Holloway's population are lone parents, and that just under half had dependent children.[4] Similarly, the National Prison Survey in 1991 found that 41 per cent of the female prison population were mothers, while HM Chief Inspector of Prisons states that in 1996 two-thirds of the female prison population were mothers of (on average) three children. Over a third of mothers had one child or more under five years of age; 43 per cent had children between five and 10 years; and 42 per cent had children between 11 and 15 years. Some 4 per cent of women had a child of up to 18 months of age in the prison with them.[5] In 10 per cent of cases in the survey of HMP Holloway conducted in 1993–1994, children had been split up from the family to be looked after by friends, and 8 per cent had been taken into care. Only 28 per cent of the children of female prisoners in this study were being looked after by their fathers, while their mothers were in prison.[6]

In short, most women who are imprisoned are convicted of non-violent, minor property offences, often committed to feed a drug habit. At the time of their conviction and imprisonment, approximately half had dependent children, and they were the primary child carers. Given these circumstances we might reasonably have expected prison

---

[3] Prison Reform Trust (1996), p. 2.
[4] *ibid.*, p. 3.
[5] HM Chief Inspector of Prisons (1997), Appendix 3.
[6] Prison Reform Trust (1996), p. 3.

to have been used sparingly as a punishment. In fact, in 1997 there were over 2,700 women in prison in England and Wales — 4 per cent of the prison population as a whole — and since 1990 the number of women being sent to prison has increased at twice the rate of men (see Table 9).

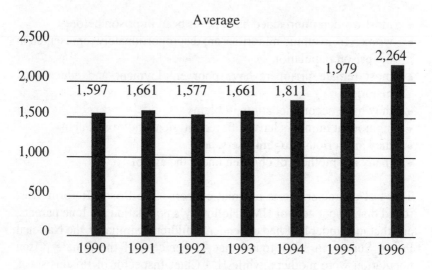

Table 9: The imprisonment of women

This chapter is primarily concerned with the experiences of women in prison. This is quite deliberate, since (as mentioned above) most evidence suggests that young women are sent to prison for less serious offences and with fewer previous convictions than men. The experience of imprisonment for women is therefore worthy of extended consideration, but it is also necessary to discuss the non-custodial options available for women who offend within our criminal justice system.

It is generally accepted that community service and probation (day) centre provision for women is inadequate.[7] Probation officers complain that they receive few female referrals, and as a consequence it is rare to find special provision for women in the form of all-female projects or groups.[8] Similarly, attendance centres for women are rare, and the number of probation and supervision orders for young women

---

[7] See A. Worrall, 'Troublesome Young Women', *Criminal Justice Matters*, No. 19, Spring 1995, pp. 6–7.

[8] For the few which exist, see C. Martin (ed.), *The ISTD Handbook of Community Programmes for Young and Juvenile Offenders*, Winchester: Waterside Press, 1997.

decreased from 2,200 in 1982 to 583 in 1992.[9] There has been a similar trend in the disposal of adult female offenders so that custody is generally used earlier in a woman's offending 'career' than in a man's. The inadequacy in this approach is underscored by the fact that young women who are remanded in custody are only half as likely as young men to receive a custodial sentence, implying that a community-based option might have been more suitable in the first place.

Cautioning is the main method of disposal used for female offenders; and while cautioning rates are high for both males and females, they have been significantly higher for young women. This perhaps reflects the fact that by and large young women commit less serious crimes than young men. As a consequence only one out of every 10 young offenders who go to court is female. The evidence relating to sentencing is confusing, but it does appear that until recently a young woman was more likely to be given a conditional discharge than a young man, and less likely to be given a custodial sentence. Things have changed over the past few years, though, and this brings us back to the recent growth in the use of imprisonment for women, and the particular experiences of women once they receive a custodial sentence.

PRISON AND THE FAMILY

When people are sent to prison, their families face a series of problems ranging from poverty and stigmatisation, to difficulties in maintaining contact with their loved ones. Even a short term of imprisonment can be disruptive, and a 1989 study found that, excluding the costs of travelling to and from the prison, families had to find on average £545 a year to support their family member in custody.[10] This figure is likely to be much higher given that prisoners can now purchase, for example, phone cards. Sometimes the demands are just too high and, according to the 1991 National Prison Survey, over half of the prisoners who had served more than five years had had a change in marital status.

We have already drawn attention to the fact that the most recent research by HM Chief Inspector of Prisons suggests that two-thirds of the women imprisoned in 1996 were mothers of (on average) three

---

[9] Worrall (1995), p. 7.
[10] Quoted in NACRO, *Prisoners' Families*, London: NACRO, 1994, p. 4.

children. Only a quarter of these children were living with their fathers and/or the mother's current spouse, compared with over 90 per cent of the children of male prisoners. Thus, the impact of imprisoning a woman is likely to cause greater damage to the family than incarcerating a man. Indeed, reflecting some of this damage, the most recent research suggests that over one in 10 women had had one or more of their children taken into care and/or fostered or adopted as a result of being imprisoned.[11]

One female prisoner, Marlene Simpson, described her experiences of being incarcerated at HMPs Bullwood Hall, Cookham Wood and Holloway. Reflecting much of the research which we have described earlier, she was imprisoned for supplying cannabis, which she sold to maintain a heroin addiction, and she outlines the difficulties she had over the course of her two-year sentence in maintaining contact with her son:[12]

Anyway the sentence had been passed and now my main concern was my son. In fact he had always been my concern from the day he was born but I had always been there to look after him ... I couldn't fully comprehend what a devastating effect [my imprisonment] would have on my son. The first few weeks of separation were unbearable. I couldn't bear to think what it was doing to John who was now staying with foster parents. The prison regime was so punitive that I could not even phone to give him a least a little comfort and reassurance that I still loved him. Visiting presented another problem.

These feelings and experiences are by no means unique. Evidence from the Partners of Prisoners and Families Support Group (POPS), based in Manchester, suggests that the circumstances described by this prisoner are very similar to those of other prisoners; but there is a variety of initiatives which could be taken by the prison service to ease the burden on families. These include:

- considering the effect on families when making decisions about where prisoners are to be allocated or transferred

[11] HM Chief Inspector of Prisons (1997), Appendix 3.
[12] All quotes are taken from the text of the article which can be found in *Scottish Child*, November 1991, pp. 22–23.

- continuing the move towards developing true 'community prisons' as recommended in the Woolf Report
- appointing a family liaison officer within each prison so as to make a member of staff responsible for coordinating resettlement plans, monitoring the quality of visits rooms, and advising on transfers
- providing clear information about visiting the prison
- being flexible about visiting times, such as allowing more visits in the evenings
- making home leave and temporary release part of a planned resettlement programme.

The first of these suggestions relates to both male and female prisoners alike, but the problem sought to be addressed is even more likely to affect women prisoners and their families given the organisation of the female prison estate in this country. On average the 1991 National Prison Survey discovered that visitors to all remand prisoners travelled 28 miles for visits, and visitors to sentenced prisoners held in local jails travelled on average 35 miles.[13] However, because there are so few prisons for women, women prisoners tend to be held at a greater distance from home than men. For example, more than half of the women at HMP Holloway in the 1993–94 survey lived outside of the London area, and almost half said that their children would not be able to visit.[14] The prisoner Marlene Simpson, quoted earlier, for example, was moved to HMP Bullwood Hall in Essex, two months into her sentence. She commented: 'John still visited but now the journey in total took eight hours. Here, John became very quiet and visibly upset when it was time to go; he even asked if he could stay with me.'[15]

Marlene was moved on from HMP Bullwood Hall to a prison in the North of England, some 300 miles from her home. Her son was now unable to visit at all. After release she described the effect of her sentence on her son:

Since leaving prison, the effect of my separation from John has become increasingly apparent. To begin with, everything seemed perfect with him, although for me, the responsibility of being a mother again was physically, emotionally, and psychologically

---

[13] NACRO (1994), p. 9.

[14] Prison Reform Trust (1996), pp. 3–4.

[15] All quotes are taken from *Scottish Child*.

taxing. I felt a huge distance between us. To protect myself I switched off so much that it felt like some of the love was missing, or at least buried very deeply. I quickly realised that I had gone away leaving, to what was for me my 'baby' and came back to find a boy I did not know much about. He had always been so open, and yet now he was very closed in. He had also had several changes of home and schools and had fallen behind in his schoolwork, even though he is a bright boy.

I would like to think that in future, particularly for non-violent offenders, alternatives to prison are more widely available, especially as it is recognised that separation between mothers and children can cause long-term damage.

WITHIN THESE WALLS — WOMEN IN PRISON

The development of the 15 prisons which hold women in England and Wales reflects the various social attitudes which we have about women generally. As we have outlined in our description of the reactions to Myra Hindley, Rosemary West and others, women who commit crimes of violence are seen as 'worse' than comparable male offenders. More typically, prisons holding women have wanted to promote regimes based on concepts such as self-help, counselling and 'domesticity', reflecting a view of women which is essentially passive. In short, these women are seen as social victims in need of help. Indeed, in 1991, a study estimated that 56 per cent of women in prison had mental health problems, although the majority did not have a definitive diagnosis of mental illness.[16] Rather they had a variety of psychological, emotional and social problems stemming from their childhood.

Yet, when asked, female prisoners will often describe a picture of their experiences in prison which belies all the evidence which we have presented. For example, most report receiving no help for the problems which they have, and only one in 10 stated that they had received any form of drug counselling. Over 70 per cent felt that prison had had a negative effect on them, allowing them to become more criminally sophisticated, angry and depressed.[17] Taken together with the evidence

---

[16] Quoted in Prison Reform Trust (1996), p. 4.
[17] HM Chief Inspector of Prisons (1997), p. 15.

that many women prisoners have accommodation problems, are mothers, have a poor employment history and are serious drug misusers, this would suggest that we need to re-think what we should do with women who are incarcerated. Instead of seeing them as either 'bad', 'sad', or 'mad', we should instead devise regimes which reflect their varied experiences and life histories.

Ten of the 15 prisons holding women are entirely dedicated to the custody of women. At the remainder — HMPs Durham, Low Newton, Winchester, Risley and Highpoint — women are located in wings which are physically separated from adult or young male prisoners, and which have their own staff. Despite the fact that staff in these 'shared sites' are specifically trained to work with women, the end result has been that, in effect, women continue to be slotted into a largely male prison estate. This causes distinct problems, especially as women do not require the higher levels of security which were introduced into prisons as a result of the Woodcook and Learmont Reports (see Chapter 2). By and large women neither riot nor attempt to escape, and the instruction to shackle pregnant prisoners during labour — since rescinded — was merely the most visible sign of a prison system designed for men, but attempting to incorporate women.

The thematic review by HM Chief Inspector of Prisons made a series of recommendations which, if adopted, would significantly alter the way in which female prisoners are accommodated, and which would tackle many of the problems which they bring with them when they are imprisoned. Despite the fact that we would go further — and we make specific recommendations regarding the use of custody for pregnant women and female juveniles — the recommendations continued within the thematic review deserve serious attention. They include:

- a recommendation to appoint a Director of Women's Prisons to have responsibility for the management of the female estate
- transitional prisons in urban counties should be developed so as to serve the re-settlement needs of female prisoners
- in determining the allocation of female prisoners, health care needs (especially the need for drug abuse treatment) and facilities for those with children should be taken into consideration
- protocols for staff dealing with visitors at prisons holding women should be developed with particular reference to behaviour as seen through the eyes of small children.

Several of the Chief Inspector's recommendations refer to prisoners who are pregnant. While we accept that if these were adopted they would significantly alter the circumstances such prisoners find themselves in, we do not believe that pregnant women should receive custodial sentences. Yet in 1996 approximately 3 per cent of women in prison were believed to be pregnant, and during 1995–96, 64 babies were born inside.[18] It is also estimated that between 1990–95, 269 babies were born to imprisoned women, and that 2,205 pregnant women had experienced imprisonment. Over 80 per cent of those who were held in prison while pregnant were incarcerated for non-violent offences, and 65 per cent of mothers had not served a previous custodial sentence.[19]

HMP Holloway is the only prison which offers pregnant prisoners the option of being located in a special part of the prison — mixing with 'vulnerable prisoners' on 'D Zero'. At other prisons women remain on normal location, unless they have a place on a mother and baby unit. More worryingly, the Howard League discovered that 63 per cent of pregnant prisoners had no access to ante-natal care, and that by and large pregnant prisoners rarely have the options available to them that they would in the community. Of note, what little ante-natal care is available inside is exclusively for the pregnant woman, and does not involve the partner of the prisoner.

There has been little research into the impact that imprisonment may have on pregnancy or the unborn child, but the Howard League concludes that pregnant prisoners 'feel stressed, anxious, frustrated and dis-empowered as a result of their imprisonment. We do not believe that this can have a positive impact on the unborn child.'[20] Given that very few women are imprisoned for crimes of violence, and that they do not pose a danger to the public, we do not believe that imprisoning pregnant women is either necessary, cost-effective or desirable.

GIRL POWER — GIRLS AND PRISON

We have described the increase in the number of women being incarcerated — twice the rate of men — and we have indicated that we

---

[18] The Howard League, *Pregnant and in Prison*, London: The Howard League, 1997, p. 1.

[19] *ibid.*, p. 2.

[20] *ibid.*, p. 9.

would attempt to unravel why this might have happened and be continuing to happen. A good place to start is to look at the experience of teenage girls. Since 1992 there has been a staggering 175 per cent increase in the number of teenage girls receiving custodial sentences, and in 1997 the Howard League found nine prisons holding girls aged under 18.[21]

Despite this, there are no establishments specially designed as young offender institutions (YOIs) for girls, and so girls sentenced to a YOI are sent to a woman's prison, partly designated as a YOI but with no suitable regime or culture for dealing with teenagers. Over 300 girls between the ages of 15 and 17 are being held in jails alongside adult women each year, directly in breach of the United Nations Convention on the Rights of the Child, and despite the fact that they are 'children' under the Children Act 1989. The Howard League also found that:

- there is little or no specialist education, work or training
- staff are largely untrained to deal with teenagers
- girls were often held a long way from home, making it extremely difficult for their families to visit
- regime provision for teenagers was extremely poor.

Adult prisoners are expected to 'mother' the girls, but this is often merely an excuse for bullying. Not surprisingly, many girls regularly harm themselves, and the threat of violence is never far from the surface. Indeed, the Howard League uncovered cases of girls mixing with adult offenders who had committed serious violent and sexual offences against children. On one occasion they discovered a 15-year-old girl who had been placed in a cell next to a woman convicted of procuring 15-year-olds for prostitution.

The Howard League interviewed 61 girls aged under 18 in 1997 who had been imprisoned. The stories they told of themselves indicated that most:

- had been subjected to physical or sexual abuse
- had drug or alcohol addictions
- had been in care

---

[21] The Howard League, *Lost Inside: The Imprisonment of Teenage Girls*, London: The Howard League, 1997, p. 7. All statistics and quotes which follow are taken from this publication.

- were excluded from school, or were long-term non-attenders
- suffered from low self-esteem.

'Bel' is fairly typical of this pattern. She had been in about 15 children's homes since the age of 14, and her longest placement had been six weeks. She had been sexually abused by her father, as had her sister and brother. Bel had a drugs problem, and took crack as it released 'the pain and anger inside'. She stole in order to buy crack, and had in fact been first placed in a children's home for her own safety because she was taking drugs. While in prison Bel had got depressed, bored, and had started to harm herself. She had also attempted suicide, and because of staff shortages was regularly locked in her cell alone for 18 hours per day.[22]

During 1996, 214 15- to 17-year-old girls were held in prison, of whom 68 per cent had been convicted of non-violent offences. Those who had been convicted of violence had largely become involved in fights with other girls who were known to them. Cases of random, violent attacks on strangers were extremely rare.

Given all of this, how do we explain the dramatic increase in the numbers of girls being sent to prison, especially as the 1990 White Paper — *Protecting the Public* — had suggested that girls under the age of 18 could be removed from the penal system altogether? It would seem two processes have been at work. The first relates to the knock-on effect of Michael Howard's 'prison works' policy, largely supported by New Labour; the second to the influence of the media.

The Spice Girls may have become popular, but in their wake the media have also started to publish stories about 'girl gangs' and 'girl violence'. An assault on the actress Elizabeth Hurley, for example, was the most visible of a spate of stories in the press, giving a completely false picture of 'girl gangs' becoming a major problem. 'Tank Girl' — a fictional, shaven-headed, beer-swilling, feminist superheroine, in biker boots and tattoos — was taken to symbolise the menace of these supposed girl gangs. The gangs — 'sugar and spice but not all nice', as *The Sunday Times* put it[23] — were seen to be not only physically threatening, but also clever and devious. As such, so we were led to believe, they were able to manipulate the criminal justice system to be

---

[22] Bel's story is told in The Howard League (1997), p. 18.
[23] *The Sunday Times*, 27 November 1994.

'soft' on them. Yet the leading expert on girl gangs has attributed all that we've just described to 'media myth making', and has declared unequivocally that 'there [is] no female gang problem in Britain': 'The Media had found a story of sex and violence and it was not going to be deterred by the fact that there is no data to suggest that British girl gangs exist in any appreciable numbers, nor that they are a new phenomenon or a growing problem.'[24]

Nonetheless, it would seem that this type of publicity has increasingly influenced our courts. Yet most of the factual evidence would suggest that girls are being imprisoned for non-violent offences, and then placed within regimes which are ill-equipped to deal with the many problems which they bring with them. We believe that the spirit of the 1990 White Paper should not be lost, and that there is little evidence to suggest the need to imprison girls under the age of 18.

---

[24] A. Campbell, 'Media Myth Making: Creating a Girl Gang Problem', *Criminal Justice Matters*, No. 19, Spring 1995, pp. 8–9.

7   Drugs

If we want to see the scale of Britain's drug problem and the failure of anti-drug policies, we need look no further than our prisons. As part of the last government's determination to 'tackle drugs together', a mandatory drug testing (MDT) programme was introduced into prisons in England and Wales in 1995. Prison seemed like a good place to start. Indeed we have already drawn attention to the number of offenders who have drug problems, and to evidence of a link between drugs and crime. The most recent research also indicates that over 70 per cent of prison officers believe that there is 'fairly extensive use' of heroin or crack cocaine in our prisons, and just under 80 per cent thought that there was 'extensive use' of cannabis.[1] Getting prisoners off drugs while in custody would in turn reduce the amount of drugs in our community when prisoners are eventually released. What is more, since the tightening of security in all prisons following the Woodcock and Learmont Reports (see Chapter 2) a wide range of technology has been introduced to prevent trafficking inside. It all seemed to make sense.

Unfortunately, things have not gone according to plan. The most recent independent research states quite boldly that 'MDT is failing on two fronts'. The first relates to the fact that there are inadequate rehabilitation programmes for those prisoners who want to come off

---

[1] M. McDonald, 'Mandating Drug Testing in Prisons', *Prison Service Journal*, January 1998, No. 115, pp. 22–25.

drugs. More worryingly, the second concerns the fact that MDT itself 'is encouraging users to switch from "soft" drugs to less easily detectable "hard" drugs'. Far from solving the problem of drugs in our prisons, or helping prisoners break their drug habits, the MDT programme has made matters worse. Indeed this new research also indicates that 'there is a high likelihood of some prisoners starting a drug habit in prison as a result of boredom or non-coercive peer pressure'.[2]

So, despite all the new technology available to prison staff, as well as old-fashioned 'sniffer dogs', within an environment which is by its very nature more controlled than the general community, a coercive, essentially punitive approach to the problem has made matters worse. Drugs are still trafficked, but they have become 'harder'; prisoners are still addicted, and end up spending longer in prison because they lose remission if they get caught; and another so-called battle in the war against drugs is essentially lost. Are there not lessons for us all in relation to our general approach to drugs in the community, based on what we know of MDT in prisons? After all, if we cannot stop drug taking inside by adopting more punitive approaches, what hope have we got of greater success outside the prison walls?

No one is pretending that any of this is easy. The drug problem is perhaps the most complex of all crime issues, because it is in fact three problems. The first relates to drug taking which, in most cases, is in that special category of crimes in which the only victim is the perpetrator. The second problem is that drugs are supplied through a vast black market in which the major players are very powerful. The third stems from the fact that in order to feed their habit, drug addicts commit a massive amount of crime, especially property crime. Any sensible drugs policy should seek to minimise the harm caused to drug users, to undermine the black market and to reduce the levels of drug-related crime. Yet all three problems have dramatically increased in recent years. This chapter will argue that the approach pursued by successive governments has failed, and that New Labour's White paper — Tackling Drugs to Build a Better Britain — merely fine-tunes some of the problems of previous approaches. Progress, we argue, can only be made through some radical and politically brave changes in policy.

---

[2] All quotes are from the research cited above.

THE DRUG PROBLEM

There can be no doubt of the validity of the general statement 'drugs cause harm', but different drugs cause different degrees of harm in different people. The drugs that do by far the most harm are legal. For example, Alcohol Concern calculates that there are over 30,000 deaths per year from alcohol related illnesses, and HEBS (the Health Education Board for Scotland) reckoned that there were over 10,000 deaths in 1995 from illnesses related to smoking.

Of the illegal drugs, at one end of the scale heroin can have a wide range of chronic and acute health effects, and kills hundreds of people a year. At the other end of the scale is cannabis. Although it can induce psychosis in some long-term, heavy users, according to a supressed passage in a recent report by the World Health Organisation, it is generally safer than alcohol or tobacco. (However, as with alcohol, people under the influence of the drug who are driving or in charge of machinery are potentially deadly.)

Deaths from the dance drug 'ecstasy' have received massive media attention, yet official estimates put the number of deaths at seven a year from the estimated half million tablets of the drug consumed each week.[3] Compare this against the number of deaths caused by adverse reactions to common pharmaceuticals, such as paracetamol, and the tabloid stories seem out of all proportion to the problem. Nevertheless, little is know about the long-term effects of the drug, and there is a growing body of medical opinion that it can cause lasting damage to the delicate chemical balance of the brain.

---

[3]Government statistics cited in K. Williamson, *Drugs and the Party Line*, Edinburgh: Pub Rebel Inc., 1997, p. 82.

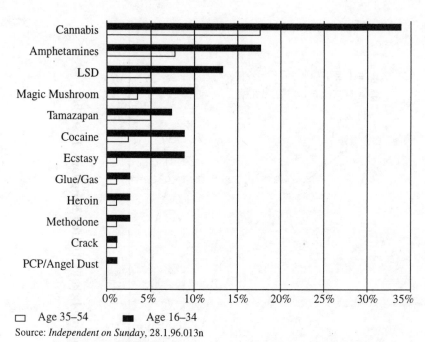

□ Age 35–54   ■ Age 16–34

Source: *Independent on Sunday*, 28.1.96.013n

Figure 3: Which of these drugs have you ever taken?

Surveys consistently show that the use of illegal drugs is widespread, particularly among young people (see Figure 3). By far the most common drug used is cannabis, which is also, in general, the least damaging. There has been an increase in drug use, and with some drugs the rise has been spectacular. 'Ecstasy', for example, was virtually unknown prior to the mid-1980s; but in 1996, 8 per cent of people under the age of 35 said that they had taken it.[4] More alarming is the rise in heroin use during the 1990s, which is thought to have been prompted by an influx of the drug which forced prices down. Throughout the 1990s the seizure of heroin has increased dramatically both in terms of the number of seizures and the weight involved (see Table 10). In 1991, 4,883 addicts were notified to the Home Office, but by 1994 that number had more than doubled to 10,067.[5] In 1979, heroin addicts made up 65 per cent of all registered addicts and 70 per cent of new addicts; by 1994, those figures had risen to 87 per cent and 93 per cent respectively.

---

[4] *The Independent on Sunday* survey, 28 January 1996.
[5] *ibid.*

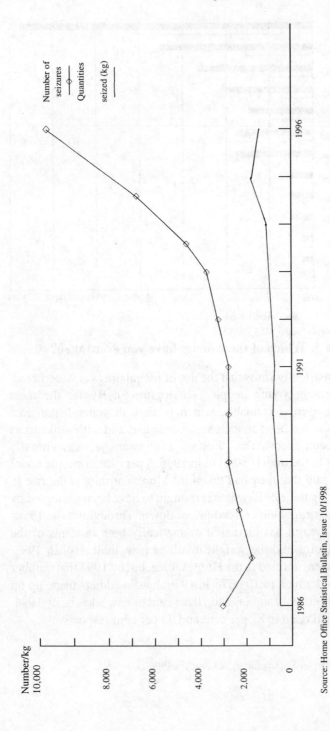

Source: Home Office Statistical Bulletin, Issue 10/1998

Table 10: Number and weight of seizures involving heroin, United Kingdom, 1986–96

Inevitably, these statistics tell only part of the story. In the experience of drug workers, as many as 90 per cent of addicts do not register with a doctor and therefore do not figure in official statistics. Frequently the anecdotal evidence provided by these workers is even more alarming than the official figures. In 1995, for example, a report by the Unit 51 drug agency in West Yorkshire stated: 'We've got something serious on our hands and we need to do something about it now. If we don't it will become an epidemic.' In January 1998, 13-year-old Allan Harper from Glasgow became Britain's youngest heroin victim.[6] Commenting on the rise in the number of young teenagers taking the drug, one of Unit 51's workers said: 'It used to send a panic around a drug agency if we saw someone so young on heroin, but it's reached the stage now where it's become normal ... heroin has become fashionable and acceptable among the young.'[7]

People found in possession of drugs for their own consumption, especially cannabis, by and large do not go to prison. In 1995, for example, over 40,000 people were cautioned for possession of cannabis, and only 930 went to prison. The rate of caution has increased dramatically over the last 10 years. In 1950, for example, only 4,048 people were cautioned for possession of cannabis, and 983 sent to prison.[8] However, even if simply cautioned, some people lose their jobs or face social stigmatisation. Repeat offenders can end up with a criminal record, and the addicts among them (particularly the heroin addicts), often end up in prison because they are unable to pay fines for repeated possession offences.

A survey of almost a thousand convicted prisoners by the Office of Population, Censuses and Surveys (OPCS) found that 58 per cent had misused cannabis in the year before imprisonment, 28 per cent amphetamines, 24 per cent LSD, 22 per cent 'ecstasy', 21 per cent cocaine (including 13 per cent crack cocaine), 20 per cent tranquilisers, 17 per cent heroin, 9 per cent methadone. Among the 21- to 24-year-olds, the level of heroin misuse was much higher at 26 per cent. Although the majority of the people surveyed were not in prison for specific drug offences, these figures show far higher levels of drug use than in the general population. Interestingly, 22 per cent

---

[6] *The Observer*, 'Death of heroin boy stuns neighbours', 25 January 1998.
[7] *The Big Issue*, 18 December 1995, cited in K. Williamson (1997).
[8] *The Guardian*, 6 February 1998.

of respondents said that they drank 'quite a lot' and 16 per cent admitted to being heavy drinkers. A separate study of remand prisoners found that 12.3 per cent of male adults and 11.7 per cent of male youths met criteria for alcohol dependence. The figures for drug dependence were 10.7 per cent and 10.2 per cent respectively.[9]

Any market, whether it be legal or illegal, involves an interplay of supply and demand. The black market in drugs is dominated by the suppliers at the top end of the chain who are able to manufacture demand by controlling prices. Despite throwing vast sums of taxpayers' money at the problem, governments have been unable to stop the market's expansion. In the five years from 1988 to 1993, for example, the US Government's drug enforcement spending rose from $4.7b to $12.3b, yet the street price of heroin and cocaine fell sharply, a sure sign that more drugs than ever were getting through the net.[10]

The same thing appears to have happened in the UK. In the 20 years between 1975 and 1995, the number of drug seizures by the police and HM Customs increased more than tenfold from just over 10,600 to 115,000; but, as the statistics cited earlier show, there have also been dramatic rises in the number of drug users, so it stands to reason that more drugs are making it on to the streets. HM Customs admit that only around 10 per cent of the heroin that comes illegally into Britain is seized by the law enforcement agencies.

In the case of cannabis, heroin and cocaine in particular, many of the most powerful suppliers are based in the Third World. Their activities do not occur in a vacuum, but rather are a reflection of the poverty and social inequality of many Third World countries. The suppliers not only have the wealth to buy political favours and military back-up, but, more importantly, they are also able to command the loyalty of the producers by providing them with a stable livelihood. As a former Detective Chief Inspector from the Greater Manchester Police's drug squad put it: 'The pressure on the poor farmers in the Third World is intense. Given the personal choice of risking seeing your children die if you plant a coffee crop, or guaranteeing a good cash return for cannabis plants or opium poppies, it is easy to see how the problems arise.'

---

[9] Drug Misusers and the Criminal Justice System', Part III of a report by the Advisory Council on the Misuse of Drugs.

[10] Figures cited in Polly Toynbee's article, 'It's a waste of money being hard on soft drug users', *The Independent*, 26 June 1997.

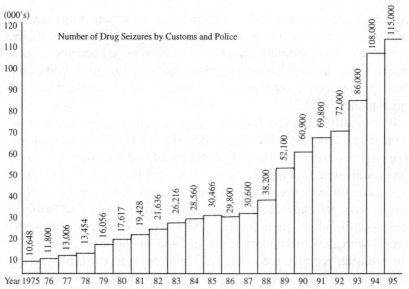

Source: Home Office Statistical Bulletins: Satistics of Drug Seizures and Offenders dealt with, United Kingdom 1975–1995.

Table 11: Number of drug seizures from 1975 to 1995

For all their anti-drug rhetoric, the western powers have, from time to time, exacerbated the situation by turning a blind eye to the activities of Third World drug barons. For example, it has recently emerged that during the mid-1980s, when Nancy Reagan, the wife of the US President, was exhorting young people to 'Just Say No' to drugs, her husband's government was colluding with some of Central America's biggest drug barons against the left-wing government of Nicaragua. It follows from all this that stemming the flow of drugs from the Third World will require profound global political and economic changes. Until that happens, the drug enforcement agencies will inevitably be fighting a losing battle.

Of course, not all drugs are produced in the poorer countries. Many, such as 'ecstasy' and amphetamines, are manufactured in laboratories in Europe. But those who control production, like their counterparts in the Third World, often possess the power and wealth necessary to corrupt law enforcement officials. Furthermore, in order to avoid incriminating themselves, they are careful to run their businesses behind a range of subordinates. Major godfathers are, of course, occasionally brought to justice, but police and Customs know that many of them have made themselves virtually immune from capture. The drug barons rely on a network of small-scale suppliers to peddle their drugs and, in Britain, as in most countries, there is no shortage of volunteers. Sadly, in a society where growing numbers of poor and poorly educated young people see a future filled with unemployment or low-paid work, drug dealing represents a relatively glamorous, if risky, means of earning quick money.

It is usually these less powerful people, further down the chain of supply, who find themselves targeted by the law enforcement agencies. The recommended sentence for people found in possession of Class A drugs with intent to supply is three to five years in prison. This includes hardened criminals who peddle heroin, but also otherwise law-abiding people who, with no intention of making a profit, buy a few 'ecstasy' tablets on behalf of their friends. The Crime (Sentences) Act 1997, passed with Labour support at the tail end of the last Conservative Government, requires mandatory minimum seven-year sentences for third-time convicted drug dealers. Locking up small-scale offenders is an expensive waste of time. It could, of course, be argued that if they were not targeted even more drugs would be consumed. There is no evidence to support this proposition and it is like saying that closing down a greengrocers will stop people buying oranges — in fact they will simply buy their oranges elsewhere. Frankly, there are simply not the resources to catch every drug dealer.

A further indication of our misguided approach to the black market is that, of the 94,000 drug offenders caught by the police, 90 per cent were arrested for possession of cannabis, the least damaging of all the major illegal drugs.[11] Likewise, of the drug offenders who were imprisoned, 80 per cent were involved with cannabis offences.[12] The estimated annual cost of their imprisonment is over £250m.

The scale of drug-related crime is staggering. A survey of 1,100 drug abusers carried out by the Department of Health found that they had committed around 70,000 crimes over a three-month period, which is an average of 64 offences each.[13] The vast majority of such crimes are property crimes carried out by heroin addicts. As we have seen, over 90 per cent of registered drug addicts are hooked on heroin. Maintaining the habit costs them each an estimated £300

---

[11] Polly Toynbee, *The Independent*, 26 June 1997.

[12] Home Office Statistical Bulletins cited in K. Williamson (1997), p. 119.

[13] Department of Health study cited by Polly Toynbee, *The Independent*, 26 June 1997.

per week and, since most addicts are unemployed, they inevitably tend to fund their addiction through crime. As stolen goods fetch only a fifth of their true value when sold on the black market, the average weekly habit may require £1,500 worth of crime. The Home Office estimates that a staggering one in five crimes is committed by heroin users, and that the total value of the items stolen each year to feed heroin addiction is £1.3b. This figure may be a substantial underestimate. A report by workers in some of Glasgow's health and drug charities estimated that that city's 8,500 heroin addicts alone commit £500m worth of crimes annually.

Heroin-related property crimes tend to be concentrated around the areas of greatest usage, which are generally the poorest areas. Thus large swathes of many towns and cities have suffered a vicious spiral of decline, the magnitude of which is not reflected in official figures and can be appreciated only if it is experienced first hand.

TACKLING THE PROBLEMS

It is our belief that the cornerstone of future drugs policy should be the decriminalisation of drug usage. Mainstream British politicians have always shied away from this bold and politically risky strategy, claiming that it will encourage further drug use. There is no evidence to support this, and common sense should tell us that people do not use drugs simply because they are legal but for a complex variety of other factors. Moreover, decriminalising drug use does not mean the legalisation of the promotion of drug taking.

In 1975, Holland became the only European country to decriminalise the usage of cannabis. If the opponents of decriminalisation were right, this should have led to a rapid rise in the usage of the drug, but over the following 10 years usage actually fell.[14] More than 20 years on, the number of cannabis users in Holland is thought to be around 675,000, which is about 4.5 per cent of the country's 15 million population. In Britain, where use and sale of the drug remains illegal, there are thought to be between six and seven million users, which is about 11 per cent of the population.

One of the main advantages of decriminalisation is that it will cease to fill up court time and result in fewer otherwise law-abiding people

---

[14] Dutch Ministry of Health Report, 'Drug Policy in the Netherlands' (1995), cited in K. Williamson (1997), p. 125.

being sent to prison, losing their jobs or facing social stigma. In addition it would make drug users, and potential users, less inhibited about coming forward to take advice on how to best reduce the harm caused by drugs. People with a serious drug problem need help and support. Although a few prisons run good rehabilitation programmes, prison, by and large, is not the best place for addicts to be, not least because many are awash with heroin and other hard drugs. Courts have the power to order offenders on to rehabilitation programmes, but rarely do. Most of these programmes are, in any case, over-subscribed, with waiting lists of around two to three months.

Ironically, the available evidence suggests that these programmes represent value for money. American research found that for every dollar spent on the programmes, $7 were saved in crime costs. A pilot study in Brighton, in which drug workers were stationed in courts and police stations in order to divert people away from prison and towards treatment programmes, found that every cured heroin addict avoided property crimes costing as much as three of the workers combined.[15] Unfortunately public spending calculations generally ignore such sophisticated accounting.

It stands to reason that the only way to defeat the drugs black market in Britain is to legalise the sale of drugs. This option is currently precluded by a number of UN agreements to which Britain is a signatory. We do not feel that legalisation would be an appropriate first step, as production of now legal drugs would be controlled by major corporations with shareholders to satisfy and a vested financial interest in having more people take drugs. A more sensible approach would be partially to legalise the sale of cannabis and to provide heroin on prescription.

Cannabis

As we have seen, cannabis is generally safer than tobacco and alcohol; it is by far the most popular illegal drug and accounts for the vast majority of drug convictions. For these reasons we believe that there is a special case for the limited legalisation of the sale of the drug. To determine how this might work we need to look again at Holland, where limited legalisation accompanied decriminalisation of cannabis usage in 1975.

---

[15] Figures cited in Polly Toynbee, *The Independent*, 26 June 1997.

The sale of cannabis in Holland is strictly regulated. It is available only at around 1,200 specially licensed premises known as coffee shops. The shops are not allowed to advertise the fact that they sell the drug (it is illegal even to have a picture of a cannabis leaf in the window) and cannot sell alcohol. The maximum purchase per customer is 5 grams, and an age limit of 18 is strictly enforced. In Britain it is often argued that cannabis should remain banned because it is a stepping-stone to more dangerous drugs, but since the coffee shops ban the sale of any other drugs, their customers are rather more insulated from this danger than they might be in the less regulated atmosphere of a British night club or party. A 1995 report by the Dutch Ministry of Health suggested that the heroin addiction rate had stabilised at a rate of 0.16 per cent of the population, but in Britain and France, where soft drug users did not enjoy the same degree of protection from heroin dealers, it was over 60 per cent higher at 0.26 per cent. Furthermore, the average age of Dutch heroin addicts has increased over the past 20 years, which suggests that fewer young people are being dragged into the habit.

The Dutch system is not a panacea. It has not seriously damaged the black market, which still dominates the supply of cannabis to the coffee shops, but it does encourage legitimate small-scale producers. The 1995 Ministry of Health report suggested that the black market might be further undermined if licences were granted to around 35,000 domestic growers, whose products could meet the current demand.

Heroin: lessons from Merseyside and Zurich

Heroin is the most problematic of drugs, not only because of the harm it does to users, but also because of the billions of pounds of crime committed by addicts. Decriminalisation of its usage alone would hardly have an impact on this phenomenon, because addicts would still need to steal to feed their habit.

From 1920 to 1967, addicts did not pose such a problem because the drug was available to them on prescription, but the Dangerous Drugs Act 1966 put an end to this system. One of the effects was to put the supply of the drug in the hands of the black market, which had a vested interest in increasing the number of users. As we have seen, since the late 1960s the number of registered addicts and the quantities of the drug seized by police and HM Customs have both risen exponentially.

However, it would be naive to suggest that Britain's heroin problem is the result of a single piece of legislation. The 30-year period since 1967 has been one of marked economic decline and corresponding social decay. The majority of heroin addicts are poor, unemployed and have few prospects. Many face further problems such as abusive childhoods, bad housing, and bringing up children single-handedly. Heroin is thus a symptom and not a primary cause of social decay, and it is only when politicians address the root causes that we can expect to see a significant decline in its usage. There are, nevertheless, a number of practical measures which could ease the immediate problems. First and foremost among them is the reinstatement of heroin on prescription, which should not be confused with the current system of prescribing methadone.

The growth of the prescribed use of methadone reflects concern about the spread of HIV among heroin users who share needles. Quite understandably, it was thought safer to provide addicts with clean needles and a drug that contained none of the impurities of black market heroin. Unfortunately methadone is highly toxic and may well kill more people than heroin. Between 1982 and 1991, for example, 243 people were recorded as being killed by heroin and 349 by methadone.[16] These figures are even more alarming when one considers that there are about 10 times as many people addicted to heroin as to methadone. An equally intractable problem is that most addicts believe methadone is a poor substitute for heroin, simply because it does not produce the same intense high. It is believed that many of those prescribed methadone sell it on in order to fund further heroin purchases.

The idea that doctors should provide addicts with heroin on prescription may seem alarming, but the only full-scale experiment to be mounted in Britain since 1967 gives cause for optimism. In 1985, Merseyside Regional Health Authority established a pilot scheme in Widnes whereby people addicted to heroin and other drugs, including amphetamines and cocaine, would be placed on a drug maintenance programme. Over the next five years, up until 1990, when political pressure forced the initiative to back-track, the police reported a 96 per cent reduction in property crime by drug addicts. This meant that fewer addicts were going to prison and so more were able to achieve much needed stability in their lives. Since the supply of heroin was no longer

---

[16] Home Office Statistical Bulletins cited in K. Williamson (1997).

controlled by criminals with a vested interest in creating more addicts, there was a reported 12-fold decrease in new cases of addiction. HIV infection from drug use was zero and there were no reported heroin deaths.[17] Despite all these local benefits, no one in the Conservative Government had the courage to advocate an extension of the Widnes experiment. It was gradually replaced by a methadone maintenance programme and eventually wound up in 1995.

During the previous year a similar experiment was introduced in Switzerland, which has some of the highest rates of heroin addiction in Europe. With a population of approximately 7 million, a report by the Swiss Federal Office of Public Health, estimated that there are between 25,000 and 30,000 heroin addicts in the country.[18] As a consequence the Swiss decided that they would adopt a radical approach to this problem. In short, they would not attempt to arrest the addicts, but rather re-shape the cashflow under which the addicts got access to heroin by making it available on prescription. By doing so they sought to eliminate the need to buy heroin on the black market with money largely obtained through crime.

This last point was very important to the Swiss in deciding to adopt the prescription project. Data from Zurich and other Swiss cities suggested the importance of drugs in explaining crime, especially muggings. Indeed it was calculated that three muggings in every four which were cleared up in Zurich had been committed by addicts in need of cash to buy drugs. So, by offering addicts legitimate access to drugs, it was hoped that there would be a substantial reduction in the rate of offending.

Preliminary results from this experiment have just been published. They suggest that there has been a dramatic reduction in aggravated forms of theft such as burglary and robbery, and that delinquency has been reduced 'to a very large extent'. The Swiss authorities are particularly pleased that drugs trafficking among those on the scheme has reduced. Over half of heroin addicts within the prescription programme used to try to obtain cash through resale of drugs to

[17] Statistics from *British Journal of Hospital Medicine*, vol. 52, No. 213, 1994, 'Drug Misuse and Social Cost'. Cited in K. Williamson (1997).

[18] All figures quoted taken from M. Killias and J. Rabosa, 'Less crime in the cities through heroin prescription: preliminary results from the evaluation of the Swiss heroin prescription projects', *Howard Journal of Criminal Justice*, vol. 36, No. 4, November 1997, pp. 424–429.

consumers from their own social network. In this way new addicts were also brought into the cycle of addiction. The Swiss would seem to have broken the link between drug dependency and the resale of drugs to new consumers. So successful has this experiment in prescribing heroin been that, in October 1997, a national referendum overwhelmingly backed the initiative — proof that bold steps need not be politically unpopular.

DRUGS EDUCATION

Successive governments have spent huge amounts of taxpayers' money telling people what they already know — that drugs are harmful — and advocating a course of action which large numbers are not prepared to follow, which is summed up in the phrase 'Just Say No'. The majority of illegal drug takers are also aware that drugs can be harmful, but, whether we like it or not, they calculate that the potential benefits make the risks worthwhile. Moreover, they know that, statistically, there is less chance of them coming to harm, for example, if they smoke a cannabis joint than there is if they smoke 20 cigarettes or go on a drinking session. The death rate from taking a single 'ecstasy' tablet has been calculated at 1:3.7m, which is around five times lower than the death rate among people who go on skiing holidays.

We should not abandon drug education as a lost cause, but need instead to ensure that it meets some very basic challenges. First, of making drug users fully aware of all the risks, in the hope that they will recognise that the benefits are simply not worth it. Secondly, to make sure that those who persist in using drugs do so in such a way as to minimise the potential harm.

Research studies suggest that the way the information is put across can be as important as the information itself. When the government-funded body Scotland Against Drugs asked a sample group of young people who they would listen to if they were considering taking illegal drugs, just 4 per cent said the media, 5 per cent the police, and 10 per cent teachers. The group that scored the best, with 37 per cent, was other young people.[19]

Many of the smaller drug agencies who work with drug users on a day-to-day basis are attuned to these realities and have risen to the

---

[19] *Scotland on Sunday* article, 22 June 1997, cited in K. Williamson (1997).

challenges admirably. They know that if they adopt the moralising 'Just Say No' approach, young people will become alienated and stop listening. Instead they follow strategies based on harm reduction which involve a non-judgemental approach and concentrate on providing detailed information about the potential dangers of drugs and about the dos and don'ts of drug taking. These agencies tend to be staffed by young people, their premises are usually relaxed and informal, and they do outreach work in venues such as youth clubs where young people congregate away from prying adults. These factors encourage young drug users to be more open about their problems and to ask more questions. Life Line agency in Manchester took its message to young night clubbers via clever cartoon leaflets featuring a spaced-out raver called Peanut Pete. In Glasgow, Enhance had DJs playing at a temporary advice shop in the city centre, which attracted around 8,500 young people in just four months.

There is a world of difference between making drug use safer and saying that drugs are safe. Yet from time to time, particularly in the wake of high-profile drug fatalities, the harm reduction approach has been criticised. The horrible irony is that the most widely reported drug fatality case of recent years, that of Leah Betts, might not have happened had the harm reduction approach been more widespread. She was a responsible young woman from a responsible family, so she would have been told that drugs were harmful and that she should not take them. Like millions of other people, she decided to ignore this message, presumably because she felt that the benefits outweighed the risks. She died after taken an 'ecstasy' tablet on her 18th birthday. Ironically her death was caused by drinking too much water, rather than as a consequence of taking the 'ecstasy'.

8   Policing

Andrew Wilford and Peter Hobson are unlikely radicals. Wilford is a public school educated furniture importer and a former Tory Party activist; Hobson is a senior executive of a major construction company and an independent member of the Bodelwyddan Town Council. Recently they've been described as looking like 'off duty policemen'.[1] They most certainly are not. In 1995, both men became so incensed by the local North Wales Police that they put adverts in the local press asking anyone who had a grievance against the force to come forward. Within a fortnight their self-styled 'Campaign for Justice' netted 81 replies, and they still continue to receive complaints at the rate of one a week.

It is difficult to imagine that such a controversy could be raging among the mountains and valleys of North Wales, because traditionally such disputes have tended to occur in London or the other large metropolitan areas. Furthermore, the people doing the complaining have often been poor and black, rather than white and middle class. Yet the problems of the North Wales police, and the dissatisfaction of people like Andrew Wilford and Peter Hobson, are merely a minor example of more general anxieties about the current state of policing in Britain.

There is a popular belief, which has been supported and encouraged by the police themselves, and in recent years by politicians, that policing is about fighting crime. In fact research tells us that policing is rarely

[1] John Ashton, 'Unreasonable Force?', *Mail on Sunday*, 8 February 1998.

about this. A study in 1971,[2] for example, demonstrated that 80 per cent of public calls to the police related to incidents which were not connected with crime. A later study[3] in Essex found that the percentage of crime-related calls varied in urban and rural communities, but that over 70 per cent of all calls were for non crime-related matters. In 1993, the Audit Commission reported that about 60 per cent of calls to a police station were not related to crime but to personal difficulties and problems, noise disputes between neighbours, missing persons or lost property.[4] Successful policing in Britain has depended on the development of an idea of the police which is about security, reliability, and dependability. Within this ideal, policing provides the only 24-hour, 365-day a year service to which the public can appeal when the normal pattern of their lives is disrupted by unexpected or unexplained events.[5]

Despite the fact that this notion of policing has taken something of a battering in recent years, it still retains a symbolic significance for a broad spectrum of the British public, which far outweighs the practical effectiveness of the service. In fact, our police are not very effective at fighting crime. By any basic criteria, our police are costly and rarely successful in catching criminals. Moreover, as we described in Chapter 1, the rate at which the police clear up crimes has steadily declined since the 1950s and now stands at around one in four. As a consequence of such facts, many in the police force seem unsure of their role[6] and feel under pressure to manage what they perceive to be their increasingly scarce resources — despite the fact that they receive the biggest share of the criminal justice system's budget. Many people are beginning to ask some searching questions about the core police function in contemporary British society.

The public especially seem to be increasingly unsure. The recent history of policing — and in particular the period from the mid-1970s onwards — heralded an era of unprecedented criticism and examination of policing in England and Wales. Similarly, in responding to a number of high-profile cases involving police malpractice, the media have

---

[2] A. J. Reiss Jr, *The Police and the Public*, New Haven: Yale University Press, 1971.

[3] M. Punch and T. Naylor, 'The Police: a social service', *New Society*, 24. 1973.

[4] Audit Commission, *Helping with Enquiries: Tackling Crime Effectively*, London: Audit Commission, 1993.

[5] For a fuller discussion of the police role, see R. Morgan and T. Newburn, *The Future of Policing*, Oxford: Clarendon Press, 1987, Chapter 5, pp. 74–103.

[6] Wolff Ollins, *A Force for Change: Report on the Corporate Identity of the Metropolitan Police*, London: Metropolitan Police (1988).

begun to focus a harsh and unflattering spotlight on allegations of police corruption, malpractice and violence. The release of the Guildford Four, Judith Ward, the Birmingham Six and the Bridgwater Four, together with the disbanding of the West Midlands Serious Crime Squad by the then Chief Constable Geoffrey Dear in 1989, represent only the most prominent of a series of events which have raised serious concerns about the direction and control of policing.[7]

More recently, the allegations surrounding the investigation of the murder of Stephen Lawrence and persistent rumours regarding the activities of corrupt Metropolitan Police Officers have all generated considerable unfavourable press coverage. These and other incidents, together with an increasingly critical portrayal of public order tactics which were forged during the miners' strike of 1984/85 and which have been refined ever since, have set the tone and fuelled public questioning and criticism. Such questioning is healthy. However, we believe that there is an urgent need for a broader public debate around what it is we want our police to do, and how they should do it. To provide a context for that debate we will sketch in the key developments in British policing in the post-war period, and will take some time in doing so, given the media myths about who our police are and what policing can achieve in our country.

FROM DIXON TO BRIXTON

The twentieth century has seen the gradual development of a type of 'community policing' which by the mid-1950s had become iconic — an ideal by which the British measured virtues such as honesty and decency. The era is characterised as the 'Golden Age of Community Policing', and is fixed in the public's imagination by the avuncular figure of PC (later Sergeant) George Dixon in the BBC TV series *Dixon of Dock Green.*

'Community policing' — or, as it is sometimes known, 'policing by consent' — is shorthand for a model of policing which is local in character, both in terms of geography and in the nature of accountability and control. On a day-to-day basis 'community policing' is defined by the essential interdependent relationship between the

---

[7] See, for example, *Independent*, 26 January 1990.

patrolling constable and the local community. The officer is dependent upon the local community for assistance and information. At the same time the police constable provides symbolic reassurance and, on occasions, practical help in dealing with relatively minor and infrequent difficulties and disturbances.

However, things began to change. A series of scandals during the second half of the 1950s, involving allegations of corruption amongst Chief Constables and a number of widely publicised allegations of malpractice by operational police officers, led to the establishment of the Royal Commission on the Police in 1959.[8] The Royal Commission reported in 1962,[9] and its major recommendations were taken on board in the Police Act 1964. The Police Act established a system of governance of policing which was to remain more or less intact for 30 years, but it did little to address some of the fundamental problems which were to bedevil the service throughout the 1970s and 1980s.

Despite a significant increase in police pay, and a general improvement in conditions of employment in the early 1960s, the service had difficulty recruiting and retaining good quality police officers during the whole of the period. The situation became so serious that in 1967 the Home Office established three working parties on Police: Manpower, Efficiency, and Equipment. The working parties reported in 1967,[10] and amongst their recommendations were details of a new policing scheme which became known as 'Unit Beat Policing' (or more colloquially the 'Panda system', after the characteristic paint scheme adopted for patrol cars). The purpose of the scheme, described in Home Office circulars, was at least in part to provide an effective incident response by police officers who patrolled in the Panda cars, and who supplemented the work of the permanent (or resident) beat officer. In practice, the need to respond to incidents, and the perennial shortage of manpower, led very quickly to the virtual abandonment of the idea of the permanent beat officer in favour of the more mobile patrol. The theory and intention behind Unit Beat Policing was sound and well-intentioned, but the manner in which it was actually introduced lacked foresight and planning.

---

[8] For a full account of the background to the Royal Commission, see T. A. Critchley, *A History of Police in England and Wales*, London: Constable (1978).

[9] *Report of the Royal Commission on the Police*, Cmd 1728, London: HMSO, 1962.

[10] *Report of the Working Party on Police Manpower, Equipment, and Efficiency*, London: HMSO, 1967.

Despite the fact that the years between 1956 and 1973 saw a gradual decrease in the number of police forces to the present 43,[11] the organisation and management of policing activities retained an essentially local character until the advent of technology. Effective radio communication with officers on foot patrol, the development of computerised systems, and the general availability of patrol cars in the late 1960s heralded an era of real change. Once police officers became mobile and communication improved, the traditional relationship that had developed with the community was no longer necessary. The radio and the fast response of colleagues in cars was now all that was required, and crime fighting became the principal focus of the patrolling constable.

Unit Beat Policing changed the character of British policing forever and, according to some observers, resulted in the politicisation of relations with the public.[12] But there is perhaps a more significant way in which the scheme affected the relationship between police and public: it is this scheme more than anything else which marks the beginnings of police professionalisation, when police officers came to see themselves as experts who could identify and respond appropriately to problems.

During the 1950s the police had steadfastly resisted any notion of characterising the service as professional. In evidence to the Willink Commission in 1959, the Police Federation said that 'There could be nothing more disastrous for relationships between Police and public than to make the Police a profession'.[13] Yet by the mid-1970s Robert Mark, the Metropolitan Police Commissioner, was enthusiastic for what he saw as the commendable change of status:

The Police are abandoning their artisan status and are achieving by the ever-increasing variety of our services and integrity, our impartiality, our accountability and our dedication to the public good a status not less admirable than that of the most learned and distinguished professional.[14]

---

[11] C. Emsley, The English Police: A Political and Social History, Hemel Hempstead: Harvester Wheatsheaf (1991).

[12] S. Holdaway, 'Changes in Urban Policing', British Journal of Sociology, vol. 28, 1977.

[13] Cited by B. Whitaker, The Police, Harmondsworth: Penguin, 1964, p. 22.

[14] R. Mark, Policing a Perplexed Society, London: Allen and Unwin, 1977, p. 42.

Despite such enthusiam, a 1982 study of a large police force found that within that context professionalism represented a 'significant problem', because it distanced police officers from the public.[15]

Publicity surrounding increasingly violent crime became more strident in the wake of the Great Train Robbery in 1963, and by the 1970s armed robbery and organised crime were perceived as a threat to society. The police began to be characterised as the 'thin blue line' holding back the rising tide of crime from the law-abiding public. Television series such as *Z Cars, Softly, Softly,* and *The Sweeney* portrayed the police as tough, uncompromising crime fighters, increasingly willing to bend the rules in an attempt to protect the public from lawlessness.[16] It is difficult to trace a direct link, but there is at least anecdotal evidence that young police officers soon saw themselves in this way.

During this period the service also had to face a growing tide of unpleasant publicity regarding the activities of some of its members. A lingering scandal surrounding corruption in the Metropolitan Police and a growing disquiet concerning police tactics and abuses of power led to what some writers describe as, 'the decline of public confidence in the Police in the 1970s and 1980s'.[17] However, much of what was being disclosed must be seen against a background of public fear resulting from rising crime and the IRA bombing campaigns of the 1970s. These campaigns resulted in both civilian and military deaths, and urgent calls for the police to catch those responsible. The public acclaim which followed the convictions of several men and women for the more notorious of these bombings only served to reinforce, in the minds of many police officers, their role as the protectors of society. Yet ironically it is precisely these convictions, and the suspicion of dishonesty in the manufacturing of evidence and other malpractice, which were ultimately to act as the focus of public concern over the state of policing.

Urban policing was becoming increasingly problematic. While Unit Beat Policing may have distanced the police from the public, the establishment of Special Patrol Groups in various forces around the country brought a much more confrontational style to the fore. Ethnic

---

[15] R. Baldwin and R. Kinsey, *Police Powers and Politics*, London: Quartet, 1982.

[16] For a fuller account of the portrayal of police in the media, see R. Reiner, *The Politics of the Police*, London: Harvester Wheatsheaf (1992).

[17] Morgan and Newburn (1987), p. 77.

minority communities had for some time been concerned by what was perceived to be the prejudiced and discriminatory way that policing was carried out in major cities, and especially in London. The frustration felt in Britain's inner cities eventually erupted, first in Bristol in 1980 and then in Brixton, Liverpool, Birmingham and Manchester in 1981, in disorder on a scale which had not been seen in Britain since the eighteenth century.

RE-ESTABLISHING POLICE–COMMUNITY RELATIONS

Commentators are agreed that the 1981 riots were a watershed for British policing, and they precipitated an urgent search for a policing framework which would rekindle the ideals of public service, integrity, reliability, and consent. In his report following the riots, Lord Scarman[18] clearly recognised the dangers inherent in the professionalisation of policing:

> They are now professionals with a highly specialised set of skills and behavioural codes of their own. They run the risk of becoming by reason of their professionalism a *corps d'élite* set apart from the rest of the community.[19]

He concluded that one of the contributory factors to the disorders was the breakdown in contact between police and public, and a lack of consultation in determining policing priorities and tactics. As a consequence Lord Scarman recommended the establishment of formal consultation processes, to provide a forum within which the police and members of the community could come together to discuss problems and solutions. However, consultative committees were intended to be more than points of contact between the police and the public. The intention behind the recommendation was that the committees would provide a focus for the development of partnerships between the police, local statutory agencies and the public. In this way a local inter-agency approach to crime problems would be developed. A number of police forces immediately adopted consultative committees after the publica-

---

[18] Lord Scarman, The Scarman Report: The Brixton Disorders, Cmnd 8427, London: HMSO (1981).
[19] *ibid.*

tion of the Scarman Report, and they were eventually enshrined in the Police and Criminal Evidence Act 1984.

Whatever the merits of the original suggestion, it soon became clear that the committees were not fulfilling their function.[20] Rather than providing a forum for discussion, they tended to become platforms for senior police officers to explain their problems and tactics to a generally supportive and unrepresentative audience made up of unelected spokespersons and special interest groups.

However, it was not only Lord Scarman who was demanding reform of the police: by 1983 the Government had begun to look at the service with a new, economic realism.

REFORMING POLICE MANAGEMENT

Policing by Objectives was essentially a customising of the management principles known as 'Management by Objectives', first developed in the late 1970s in the United States.[21] Although their book was never published in this country, Lubans' and Edgar's work proved to be highly influential in determining the direction of police management through the 1980s and 1990s. This influence depended on two factors. First, it was taken as a model by some very influential senior police officers, notably Sir Kenneth Newman, who at the time was Head of the Police Staff College. Secondly, and possibly more importantly, the Home Office and the Treasury saw the potential of this style of policing for bringing a degree of financial accountability to the service. As such, in 1983 the Home Office issued Circular No. 114,[22] which began the process requiring the police to consider the costs and outcomes of their operations.

Policing by Objectives in fact marked the real beginning of a managerial approach to policing, and has served as the blueprint for the development of the new 'managerialism'. At first the police service did not adapt easily to this new discipline. The organisational principles,

---

[20] See, for example, S. Savage and C. Wilson, 'Ask a Policeman, Community Consultation in Practice', *Social Policy and Administration*, vol. 21, No. 3, 1987.

[21] V. A. Lubans and J. M. Edgar, *Policing by Objectives*, Hartford, Conn.: Social Development Corporation, 1979.

[22] Home Office, *Manpower Effectiveness and Efficiency in the Police Service*, Circular 114/83, London: Home Office, 1983.

structures and ideologies which had been in place virtually unchanged since Victorian times, had created a mechanistic approach to management which was not sufficiently flexible to deal with the complex demands which were being placed upon the service.

The police had also to take into account the findings of the Audit Commission, which since 1982 has been publishing a series of police papers which focus on different aspects of police performance and management. At first these papers were accepted (if not welcomed) by the service because they looked at peripheral activities such as vehicle fleet management, but gradually they began to focus on mainstream policing activities. In 1990, for example, the Commission published Paper No. 8,[23] which highlighted 'serious shortcomings in police management style, vision and leadership'.

This paper had a significant impact on the service, and acted as a catalyst for change. Chief Constables could no longer rely on old-fashioned managerial practices — the service had to begin to recognise the need for an open-minded approach in which management was seen to be as effective as in any private sector organisation and focused on results rather than activity. It was no longer sufficient to demonstrate that the police were busy: it was important to know what they were achieving by way of, for example, clear-up rates.

At the same time senior government ministers had become impatient with the police. They felt that they had invested large sums of money in the service and yet crime figures continued to rise and detection rates were falling.[24] By the time John Major won the 1992 General Election there was general agreement in the Government that the police were ripe for reform. The new Home Secretary, Kenneth Clarke, who had been responsible for many of the reforms of the Health Service in the latter part of the 1980s, immediately set up an internal Home Office review of the police service which was eventually published as the Police Reform White Paper.[25] This was followed by an independent enquiry into police pay and conditions of service, known as the Sheehey

---

[23] Audit Commission, Effective Policing: Performance Review in Police Forces, London: HMSO (1990).

[24] K. Baker, The Turbulent Years: My Life in Politics, London: Faber & Faber, 1993, p. 450.

[25] Home Office, Police Reform: A Service for the Twenty First Century, Cmd 2281, London: HMSO, 1993.

Enquiry[26] after its Chairman, and by a Home Office review of police core and ancillary tasks (the Posen Enquiry).[27]

After a great deal of controversy, many of the more radical proposals of the Sheehey Enquiry were quietly dropped by Michael Howard who succeeded Kenneth Clarke as Home Secretary. After a very stormy passage through the House of Lords, some of the principles of the Police Reform White Paper and the remaining Sheehey recommendations were enacted as the Police and Magistrates' Courts Act 1994. This piece of legislation made major changes to the structure of police management and accountability, and required police forces for the first time to publish an annual policing plan. Such plans are formulated with consultation in the community and form the basis of policing policies for the year. It is against these plans that police budgets will be set and performance will be measured.

So at the end of all this we can see that there have been genuine attempts to re-organise the police. The bureaucratic, centralised organisation of the 1970s and 1980s has been replaced by locally accountable basic command units; managerial structures have been flattened; and senior police officers are now required to justify their policies with results. Typically there is now a geographic policing model which allocates a group of officers to respond to calls from the public on a 24-hour basis. Other officers are posted to sectors or areas where they work flexible hours to suit the needs of the area. In doing so the hope is that they form part of the community, responding to problems and developing links. But has this really happened?

RETHINKING THE FIGHT AGAINST CRIME

It was not only police organisation and management that was perceived to be in need of reform. Increasingly during the 1980s and 1990s, the fight against crime began to be characterised as 'a problem' and something 'had to be done'. Inevitably this led to a redefinition of the police role; to an increase in police powers; and to an overhaul of police practices.

---

[26] Sir Patrick Sheehey, *Report of the Enquiry into Police Responsibilities and Rewards*, Cmd 2280, London: HMSO, 1993.

[27] Home Office, *Review of Police Care and Ancillary Tasks: Final Report*, London: HMSO, 1995.

The 1980s saw the rise of the small-time criminal and the almost casual and disorganised involvement of young men in crime for gain and excitement. Burglary, car theft and street robbery (mugging) became not only a fashion but almost a requirement. Fuelled in the eyes of some commentators by unemployment and drugs, the 'epidemic of crime' seemed to be in danger of 'engulfing' our society. Reports of crime with colour photographs, and descriptions of victims' injuries in the press and on TV, heightened public awareness to unprecedented levels. A number of horrific crimes, such as the murder of James Bulger and the Dunblane killings, further contributed to the creation of a fear of crime out of all proportion to the risks of becoming a victim.

Perhaps as a consequence we have also seen a hardening of attitudes to alternative life-styles, which has resulted in the criminalisation of a variety of modes of living and conduct. While disruptive, inconvenient and sometimes distasteful, such life-styles have never really presented a serious threat to British society, and in most cases could have been better dealt with by other courses of action. Hippies and New Age travellers, for example, characterised as inconsiderate, dirty and sometimes criminal, became a particular problem principally because some found ways to manipulate and defraud the social security system. It is doubtful if the police powers granted in the Criminal Justice and Public Order Act have had any but the most marginal effects on their activities. Along the way the same Act gave the police powers to deal with environmental protesters, squatters and the organisers of rave parties.

No one is suggesting that these activities should have been allowed to go unchecked, only that giving more and more power to the police, and demanding ever greater results, is not the best or most effective way to proceed. Indeed the evidence is that most police forces have exercised considerable common sense in using the new powers, and have not by and large involved themselves in direct confrontation with protesters and other groups. The actions of Thames Valley Police in dealing with the Newbury by-pass protesters, for example, show that difficult situations can be handled without resort to Draconian criminal law remedies in what are essentially civil protests.

Neither can it be denied that there is a fear of crime in our society. Often this fear is born out of the all too frequent experience of ordinary people of burglary and car crime; of minor vandalism and the activities of seemingly uncontrolled youth on our streets. It is also true that everyday 'minor property offences' are in fact serious offences to the victims who are deprived of their possessions, their vehicles, and their sense of security.

In response, everyone, including the police, is searching for a cause and a solution. As we argue in Chapter 9, drugs are now identified as a major contributory cause of crime in our cities. Indeed, most young men sentenced to a term of imprisonment have some form of drug habit. It is also true that the recreational use of drugs by young people is now well established, and there is evidence that a great deal of theft is committed to provide money for drugs. The police have responded by increasing the emphasis being placed on the detection and prosecution of drug traffickers, with increased powers and growing cooperation between the police, HM Customs and Excise and the security services. The soon-to-be-launched National Crime Squad will have drugs as one of its priorities once it commences operation. It is also no coincidence that the new 'Drugs Tsar' is a former policeman.

The increased cooperation between services is an example of an approach to crime known as 'intelligence led policing'. This has been adopted by police forces throughout the country. Intelligence led policing focuses not on the crime, but on the known criminal, building up a comprehensive body of evidence which it is hoped will eventually enable successful prosecutions and the recovery of quantities of stolen property and/or drugs. Among the well-known examples of this approach is 'Operation Bumble Bee', an operation against persistent burglars and receivers of stolen property, initially in London but later successfully extended to a number of forces throughout the country. However, the best known policing initiative of all is 'zero tolerance'.

ZERO TOLERANCE AND BEYOND

Despite everything we have described in this chapter, crime remains a problem, and we still expect our police to do something about this. Consequently, as has so often happened in the field of criminal justice, we have turned to the USA to find a solution — 'zero tolerance'. This is one of the more recent and controversial approaches to the problem of crime in the inner city. It was developed by William J. Bratton in New York, and has subsequently been adopted in a number of cities in the USA and Britain. In essence zero tolerance is based on a belief that there is a link between civil disorder and crime; and that, for example, by replacing broken windows, or removing graffiti and litter, a neighbourhood will become more orderly and law-abiding.

The most prominent examples of zero tolerance policing in Britain have been in Hartlepool and Middlesborough in the Cleveland force area, although there have been smaller-scale trials in other cities. We know more about the approach in Hartlepool and Middlesborough because of the missionary zeal of its most prominent advocate — Detective Superintendent Ray Mallon — and his ability to generate publicity and support. Indeed, Mallon famously promised to resign if he did not cut crime by 20 per cent in 18 months. This remark earned him the nickname 'Robocop'.

A great deal is claimed for zero tolerance policing, but it is the apparent fall in crime rates which is used as evidence to support its claims for success (Mallon did indeed cut recorded crime by a fifth). However, despite some very approving publicity, the system is not without its problems, and in December 1997 Mallon was suspended as Head of Middlesborough CID. Those who support the zero tolerance approach often justify it by looking back to the 'Golden Age of Policing' with something akin to longing.

In fact, despite claims to the contrary, zero tolerance as practised in New York and in Hartlepool and Middlesborough looks much more like intolerant policing than confident policing. The approach, with its relentless focus on targets, may indeed reduce crime in the short term, but it carries with it risks over time. Not only might some feel it in their interests to manipulate statistics in the drive to meet targets, but also some sections of the community will feel victimised and alienated.

While the targets are easy — the vagrants, glue sniffers, and graffiti sprayers — the approach can seem to produce dramatic results. Only the most naïve and inexperienced police officer would deny that the underclass of the socially disadvantaged, the disaffected and the feckless, motivated by a desire for excitement, alcohol or drugs (or a combination of all three), is responsible for much minor and some serious crime. Removing those elements from the streets, or displacing them to another neighbourhood, is bound to have an effect on crime and social order. The publicity surrounding zero tolerance has highlighted apparent dramatic success in reducing crime, but drink, drugs, unemployment and social disadvantage are related to criminal and anti-social behaviour in a very complex way. It is difficult to isolate the effect of any particular policing strategy and relate it directly to an apparent fall in reported crime. In fact reported crime fell throughout the USA and Britain, and in areas without zero tolerance policing.

In any event, would we want to live in a society where we required our police to eliminate crime altogether? There is a general acceptance that attempts to do so would create an oppressive and totalitarian environment which would be unacceptable in a liberal democracy. It is perhaps also worth noting that there have been various aggressive policing policies adopted in the past, both in the USA and in Britain, in an attempt to deal with previous 'crime problems'. Indeed it was aggressive policing which lit the fuse to Brixton's disorders in 1981. In a discussion of innovative policing strategies, criminologist Professor Robert Reiner reviewed the empirical evidence relating to a number of differing policing styles, including what he describes as 'aggressive patrol', and concluded: 'The British Police have broadly accepted Lord Scarman's message that any marginal gains in law enforcement due to aggressive tactics are not worth the cost in endangering public tranquillity.'[28]

'Policing' is a term which many think they understand, but which is incredibly difficult to define. Police officers at all levels, politicians and academics have spent a significant proportion of the past 30 years attempting to agree a satisfactory definition and description which effectively encompasses all that the police do — within the context of the need for economy and efficiency and effectiveness in their operations. However, to some extent these two needs are incompatible; and that's the problem. If the police role is to be defined primarily in relation to 'crime', performance should be judged by crime prevention and detection. However, other more symbolic functions of policing will be in danger of being neglected, and the public will become less satisfied and less supportive. This in turn will make the crime fighting role more difficult. If, on the other hand, the service role of the police is to be emphasised, and the ability to respond to all manner of undefined and unpredictable events is to be preserved, a degree of inefficiency and unproductive activity must be tolerated.

Just as the old-style rigid, militaristic leadership of the 1950s could not cope with the need to change in the 1960s and 1970s, the new managerialism is in danger of becoming equally rigid and doctrinaire in

---

[28] Reiner 1992 Op. Cit.

its relentless pursuit of performance targets. There is already anecdotal evidence that in some areas the sector policing units, set up as part of the new geographically based policing schemes, are being denuded of officers to ensure that the response units are fully manned at all times. This enables them to deal efficiently with public calls for assistance so that performance targets can be achieved. There is a real danger that the mistakes of Unit Beat Policing will be repeated 30 years later.

What then of the future? We are undoubtedly moving towards a nationalisation of serious crime investigation. The National Crime Squad will operate across force boundaries. It will have its own Police Authority; and while it will cooperate with local Chief Constables, its operational head (the National Coordinator) will have operational autonomy.

We will also have two-tier policing. On the one hand, serious crime will be dealt with by elite national bodies; on the other hand, minor property crime, burglary, street robbery, woundings and domestic murders will remain the province of local police forces. The danger is that the police will become even more remote and the public increasingly dissatisfied. It takes vision and strong leadership to build on the undoubted skill and professionalism of the British police, and the strong support of most of the British people. That leadership must come not from the police themselves, but rather through reasoned debate. Ordinary people must be able to contribute to that debate through local and national political institutions, and through a proper objective analysis of problems and potential solutions which are discussed and agreed by those who have the most to lose.

The British police are still regarded as the model to be copied by societies around the world. We should endeavour to develop from this base — a base which relies partly on tradition, but also partly on the fact that even in these troubled times when the police are seen to be less than perfect, and the public are more questioning than at any time in our history, they are still viewed as a generally reassuring rather than a threatening presence. However, we also have to accept that the real way to 'fight' crime is rarely in the hands of our police, no matter what we see on *The Bill*.

9 Probation and Alternatives to Prison

In the autumn of 1997, Jon Silverman, the BBC's Home Affairs correspondent, chaired a conference on behalf of the Essex probation service. His opening remarks neatly summarised the position which the probation service nationally finds itself in at the end of the century — 'you live in interesting times'. He hardly needed to remind his audience that this phrase stems from a Chinese curse. These 'interesting times' have resulted in the probation service having to make profound changes to its working methods, structure and organisation. In doing so, and partly as a consequence, it has had to fight off attempts to swamp its personnel with soldiers leaving the Army; agree to the abolition of its traditional social work qualification; and participate in discussions to establish a closer working relationship with HM Prison Service. Indeed, there are almost daily rumours that the two services will unite and change their name to the 'Corrections Service'. Is it also significant that Joyce Quin MP is the first joint Minister for Prisons and Probation? Why all of this has happened, and more importantly whether any of these changes and proposals will make our country safer, is the focus of this chapter. We begin by looking at the origins and development of the probation service.

THE HISTORICAL ROOTS OF PROBATION

During the mid-nineteenth century magistrates and judges in some of Britain's courts started to look for ways of avoiding the harsh mandatory sentences that they were required to pass. In some cases they began to accept the help of volunteers, sponsors and employers to act informally as supervisors of the offenders. In 1876, as this trend was spreading, a Hertfordshire printer called Frederick Rayner made a donation to the Church of England Temperance Society in the hope that something might be done about the large number of drunks who were daily paraded before the London police courts. The society responded by appointing a number of missionaries who were tasked with interviewing drunks in the court cells, evaluating those who were likely to respond to help, and suggesting to the court a plan which would provide an alternative to prison and put these 'sinners' back on the 'straight and narrow'. The plan, which the missionaries undertook to oversee, usually involved a temperance pledge, living in a supervised hostel and searching for gainful employment.

As the movement spread it was discovered that the police court missionaries could have a positive effect on a wide range of offenders besides drunks. The Government of the day recognised the merits of the system and in 1907 passed the Probation of First Offenders Act, which enabled courts to release offenders on probation, having taken into account the circumstances of the offence, the offender's character and his or her past history. The missionaries' work was regarded as so successful that the 1907 Probation of Offenders Act, which made probation available to all courts, was passed virtually unopposed.

The Act did not make probation a sentence of the court in its own right, but rather an opportunity for the offender to mend his or her ways without being sentenced to one of the punishments available to the court. If he or she breached the probation order, the original offence could be reinstated and a sentence passed. The primary duty of the missionaries, or probation officers as they became known, which was enshrined in the Act, was to 'advise, assist and befriend' the offender. Thus the probation service was founded on principles of welfare, rather than punishment.

A CHANGING SERVICE

During the twentieth century the probation service gradually came under the control of the Home Office. At the same time it continued to expand and adapt. Besides its original role of providing adult offenders with welfare orientated alternatives to prison, it was finally given, via various Acts of Parliament, the following responsibilities, many of which were undertaken informally well before the relevant legislation:

- the supervision of juvenile offenders
- the production of social enquiry reports into offenders (now called pre-sentence reports) for the courts
- the aftercare of prisoners released early on parole licence
- prisoners' welfare
- providing accommodation for offenders
- the welfare of children in family legal proceedings.

Although this chapter refers to 'the probation service', it is in fact made up of 55 area services in England and Wales, most of which are county based. During the late 1960s there was strong pressure for the functions of the probation service to be undertaken by new, expanded, county council social services departments. These moves were successfully resisted by the probation officers in England and Wales, but the Social Work (Scotland) Act 1968 led to a merger north of the border which began in 1969. The probation service in the south maintained a strong welfare ethos, and probation officers were required by law to have a social work qualification. However, whereas social workers were generally closely supervised, probation officers dealt with their clients largely as they chose, and they remained personally responsible to the court for the conduct of each case.

The introduction of parole and supervision of life sentence prisoners in 1967 prompted an important shift in the role of probation officers. From this time they were now charged with assessing the risk posed by very serious offenders, and with supervising them for an average of 10 years. In the 1970s the pressure to step up this policing role grew as law and order became a major political issue. The independence which most officers regarded as essential began to be attacked by both the left — who complained that much of the officers' work was oppressive towards their clients and stigmatised them — and the right — who demanded tougher sentencing and cited research findings which seemed to suggest that probation did little or nothing to prevent people re-offending.

Perhaps the most significant shift came with the introduction of community service. This is a sentence of the courts which involves the offender carrying out unpaid work, under the supervision of a probation officer, on projects which are beneficial to the community. Politicians viewed community service as an attractive option because it blended punishment and reparation. Ideally it also brought about the rehabilitation of the offender. However, it did not provide him or her with help in tackling the long-term problems which may have underlain his or her criminal behaviour. So, for probation officers, community service represented a further step away from their primary role as providers of social welfare, and a further move towards becoming agents of punishment. The shift foreshadowed what was to come.

During the early 1980s, in the wake of the 1979 election victory of Margaret Thatcher, whose popular appeal was partly based on her promise to pursue vigorous law and order policies, the probation service enjoyed an unprecedented increase in resources. However, at the same time, it faced increased political pressure to relinquish its perceived role as 'the criminal's friend'. Elsewhere in the world, most notably in America, probation was shifting away from the rehabilitation of offenders, towards monitoring and controlling them. The Criminal Justice Act 1982 heralded a similar shift, as it empowered the courts to impose specific restrictions on offenders as part of probation orders. Subsequent Home Office policy documents called for managerial reforms which would ensure that resources were being deployed efficiently, and that the effectiveness of the service could be clearly measured.

Rank and file probation were largely hostile to such initiatives, and its representatives pointed out that rigid performance measures could not be applied to the subtle and complex human interactions that lay at the heart of their work. Nevertheless, some probation areas began to develop practices in line with Home Office thinking. These included the adoption of intensive group work, rather than traditional one-to-one case work, and the involvement of probation officers in bail and remand decisions.

As the profession wrestled with its conscience, the Government began to discuss measures which would further undermine probation officers' traditional role. In 1987, for example, the House of Commons Home Affairs Committee recommended that the Home Office should investigate whether electronic tagging might be introduced for petty offenders. At around the same time Government ministers let it be known that they were considering transferring responsibility for probation services to voluntary and private sector organisations which would have none of the ideological difficulties in adapting to the new demands.

THE PROBATION SERVICE IN THE 1990s

The extension of punishment in the community

Despite its desire to been seen to be tough on crime, by 1990 the Conservative Government was persuaded that locking up offenders, in the words of Home Secretary David Waddington, was 'an expensive way of making bad people worse'. As we described in Chapter 1, the Criminal Justice Act 1991 attempted to divert offenders away from prison. Central to the new thinking was the formalisation of the notion, first seen with community service, of 'punishment in the community'. In effect the offender's liberty would be restricted by means of a 'community sentence' rather than by imprisonment. Besides community service, the options available to the court sentencing those whose crimes were deemed, in the words of the Act, to be 'serious enough', were:

- standard probation
- probation with added conditions, such as living at an approved hostel or attending a drug or alcohol treatment course
- a combination order, which is probation plus community service, plus, in some cases, added conditions such as those above
- a curfew order.

Since it was responsible for the provision of community sentences, the probation service was to take up a central role in the criminal justice system. Furthermore, since the Act demanded that the courts should sentence offenders according to the crimes they had committed, rather than on their criminal records, it was clear that significantly fewer people would be sentenced to prison and more would be given probation. No doubt in anticipation of this development, the Act set out the service's statutory purposes as being (i) to secure the rehabilitation of the offender; (ii) to protect the public from serious harm from the offender; and (iii) to prevent the commission by him or her of further offences. Although it did not say so in as many words, this meant a further withdrawal of the probation officers' original role of advising, assisting and befriending the offender, and an extension of the policing role.

The rise of the managed service

A further provision of the 1991 Act, and an echo of the hints that had been dropped by ministers since the late 1980s, was the introduction of formal partnerships between the probation service and other bodies, including ones from the voluntary and private sectors. A number of organisations, such as the National Association for the Care and Resettlement of Offenders (NACRO) and the National Children's Homes (NCH), had well-established schemes for dealing with offenders, but the Act required local probation services to allocate up to 5 per cent of their budgets to the independent sector. Many probation officers felt that this would require them to spend less of their time working directly with offenders and more of it coordinating their resources and assessing whether or not they were abiding by the conditions of their court order.

This specific change was merely one of many amid the continuing management orientated shift which the probation service, in common with much of the public sector, had been undergoing since the 1980s. Among the other significant stages in this transformation were the development of an overall 'Statement of Purpose' for the service, and the publication of the 'National Standards for the Supervision of Offenders in the Community'. These cover such areas as pre-sentence reports, and probation, community service and combination orders.

Few would argue that the service needs a coherent set of aims and standards by which its performance can be measured, but such changes also inevitably increase the amount of bureaucracy in the service, and further reduce the amount of time that officers can spend working with offenders. Figure 4 explains in summary form the major changes undergone by the probation service during the period under discussion.

Probation: traditional	Probation: changes
• a hard working, loose-knit organisation with high ideals	• a more managed service with an emphasis on measured activities
• single probation officers working with individual offenders	• main offender supervision in groups. Individual supervision retained for the most dangerous offenders
• high case loads	• casework prioritised on the basis of risk assessments
• probation work undertaken largely unmeasured in relation to effectiveness	• greater emphasis on research and evaluation

Figure 4: The changing face of probation

The effect of 'law and order' politics

The Criminal Justice Act 1991 did not have universal support within the Conservative Government. David Waddington's successor as Home Secretary, Kenneth Clarke, abolished the system of unit fines; thus the role of the fine as the primary non-custodial sentence was seriously undermined, which inevitably had a knock-on effect for the probation service. Clarke's 1993 Criminal Justice Act also played to the law and order gallery by allowing the courts to take into account offenders' previous criminal records when passing sentence.

Yet Kenneth Clarke was liberal when compared to his successor, Michael Howard. Howard resolved from the outset to introduce hard-line criminal justice policies, based on prison and punishment rather than on the community and rehabilitation. When he promised in 1993 to 'correct the thirty year in-built bias in favour of the criminal and against the protection of the public' it must have been clear to most probation officers that Howard was making a thinly veiled attack on their profession. Significantly, he redirected resources towards the prison system and he and his ministers cited research which indicated that prison was just as effective as probation and community service in reducing offending.

This political initiative was given momentum by a series of media stories suggesting, among other things, that so-called 'bail bandits' were running amok and that young offenders were being rewarded for their criminality. In 1994, for example, the tabloid press revealed that Gloucestershire social services had sent a 17-year-old offender on a £7,000 'character building' African safari trip. Such stories made no distinction between local authority social service schemes and programmes run by the probation service.

In 1995, Howard presented a new blueprint for community sentences, which restricted the discretion that probation officers were allowed to exercise in dealing with their clients, and transferred the power to specify the content of community services from the probation service to the courts. A dramatic shake-up of recruitment and training procedures was also announced to replace what Howard characterised as a 'liberal do-gooding ethos'[1] with a disciplinarian approach. Control of probation training was to be removed from higher education establishments, and the legal requirement for probation officers to have a social work qualification was removed. These changes were backed up with calls for the probation service to recruit ex-servicemen and ex-police officers, who would be steeped in a culture of discipline and obedience rather than social work values. In fact the service has always drawn many recruits from these occupational groups.

Howard also indicated an enthusiasm for the introduction of performance-related pay for probation officers, based on such measures as the number of probation orders successfully completed and the reconviction rate of offenders. The idea was condemned by the profession as impractical and unworkable.

Howard's parting shot, the Crime (Sentences) Act 1997, voted through with Labour Party support shortly before the 1997 General Election, which imposed mandatory prison sentences for certain categories of offenders, further demonstrated the Home Secretary's lack of faith in the rehabilitative potential of probation.

Jack Straw, Howard's Labour successor, has shown little sign of back-tracking from his predecessor's approach. Although his Crime and

---

[1] *The Guardian*, 27 July 1994.

Disorder Bill promises an extension of non-custodial sentences for young offenders, other plans, such as increased supervision of sexual and violent offenders who are released from prison, may herald a further emphasis on control of crime rather than on rehabilitation of offenders. (Such measures do, however, recognise the probation officer's role in managing the risk posed by these offenders.) A further indication of Straw's leanings are the reports that he has considered changing the probation service's name to the 'Corrections Service', in order to demonstrate his determination that probation should not be viewed as a soft option.

The Home Secretary has also given the go-ahead to private sector involvement in probation. Group 4 Security has been awarded a contract to fill welfare officer posts at the new Altcourse prison in Merseyside, which is due to open in 1998. The welfare officers will wear uniforms, and will occupy jobs which would otherwise have gone to probation officers. Similarly he announced a new training qualification for those wanting to become probation officers, which would focus on the 'integrated approach' of working with offenders and 'on probation's top priority role of protecting the public and reducing crime through effective work with offenders'.[2]

WHO IS ON PROBATION?

The probation service probably has the lowest profile and is the most disabled of all the agencies within the criminal justice system. Yet it currently has over 150,000 people under its supervision, which is well over twice the number of people in prison. The service has had to cope with rapid change. Of those 117,300 formally on probation at the end of 1997, over 40 per cent now have a previous custodial history. This is more than double the number in the late 1970s. In that same time span the number of offenders under supervision who have been convicted of burglary, robbery or another indictable offence, has risen from 28 per cent to over 50 per cent, while the number of offenders under the age of 21 has dropped from around 50 per cent to around 20 per cent. In 1996 the probation service dealt with 115,000 offenders on court orders and a further 42,000 on pre- and post-prison supervision; 218,000 court

---

[2] Parliamentary Written Answer No. 255, 29 July 1997.

reports were provided for criminal proceedings, as well as nearly 37,000 family court reports and 10,600 mediations. All this was achieved by 7,300 staff, which is 6 per cent fewer than at the end of 1994.

The 1991 Criminal Justice Act has meant that probation officers now have to supervise far more offenders who are deemed to be at high risk of committing further crimes. In 1994 HM Inspectorate of Probation was surprised to learn that at any one time there were 14,000 people under supervision who represented a potential risk of serious harm. Inevitably many of those on probation face acute social problems: over 80 per cent are unemployed, more than half are drug or alcohol abusers, and there are significant minorities with mental health and housing problems. Despite all these pressures, 80 per cent of probation orders are completed without the offender being reconvicted or breaching the requirements of the supervision order. Just 9 per cent are terminated following a further conviction.

Probation undoubtedly represents value for money. It costs £2,510 a year to supervise a probation order and £1,840 pa to supervise someone on community service. This compares to the £24,000 or more that it costs to keep someone in prison for a year.

There have been three main pieces of research demonstrating the effectiveness of probation: the Kent Reconviction Study in 1991; the Cleveland Study undertaken by the University of Durham; and the Inner London Probation Service's study of the Camberwell Probation Centre. The Kent Reconviction Study tracked 857 offenders subject to probation supervision over a period of five years and anticipated — on the basis of Home Office research — that 56 per cent of this group would normally be reconvicted. Yet, as a result of probation intervention, only 48 per cent were reconvicted. The study also demonstrated a link between drug abuse, poverty and unemployment, and those offenders most likely to become reconvicted.[3]

The Cleveland Study used a smaller number of offenders, but confirmed the general pattern uncovered in the Kent research in that community-based interventions were found to be more effective at stopping people committing crimes than sending them to prison. Similar overall results were produced by the Inner London Probation Service's study of the Camberwell Probation Centre, but it should be remembered

[3] M. Oldfield, *The Kent Reconviction Study*, Kent Probation Service, 1991. All the research quoted in this section was used at the Essex Probation Conference, 18 September 1997.

that all three studies have been rather limited in their scope and have had some contradictory findings. Nonetheless, comparing offenders who receive a prison sentence with those who commit similar offences but are given probation suggests different reconviction patterns, and that probation is much more effective (see Table 12).

Age	Prison	Probation
17–20	84%	70%
21–25	77%	53%
26–30	50%	41%
Over 30	43%	26%
All ages	72%	48%

Table 12: Reconvictions of offenders sentenced at magistrates' courts (Kent Study)

Recently a more wide-ranging study on the effect of probation was conducted by Greg Mantle of Anglia Polytechnic University, at the request of the Essex Probation Service. Mantle's findings suggest that most offenders who complete a probation order are likely to have perceived its purpose in terms of reducing the likelihood of their re-offending. Indeed, two-thirds of those surveyed felt that their probation order had actually achieved this purpose 'very much' or 'considerably', and that probation was largely seen as being about 'control' rather than 'welfare'. The main findings of the research were:

- that offenders felt that the key purpose of the probation order is to prevent re-offending
- two-thirds of participants reported that probation had reduced considerably their chance of re-offending
- a return to court was recognised as the inevitable consequence of failing to keep appointments
- 71 per cent found their contact 'helpful' or 'very helpful', and fewer than 1 in 10 felt that it had not been helpful at all.

GOOD PROBATION PRACTICE

The Essex Motor Project

The Essex Motor Project was established in 1993 to deal with young car offenders, and its two centres in Colchester and Basildon are among about 60 currently operating across England and Wales. Participants are referred to the project on the recommendation of probation officers as part of a court order, and they participate in a specified number of weekly sessions, which vary according to the requirements of the order.

Typically the offenders will have begun committing car crimes at the age of 14 to 15, and by the time they reach the project many believe they have achieved status from their crimes and display addictive behaviour. Most have been disqualified from driving, and some have already spent time in prison. All of this usually prevents them from being able to afford the insurance cover necessary for them to drive legally. Thus they are frequently locked into a pattern of repeat offending.

Under the supervision of experienced professionals they learn basic motor mechanic skills while preparing donated cars for banger racing. By regularly attending the sessions the offenders become more disciplined, and working in groups tends to give them a sense of team spirit. Hand in hand with this practical work they receive counselling in victim awareness, decision making, attitudes, self-image and self-esteem, all of which stress the benefits that can be gained by giving up crime.

One of the group — usually the one who shows most endeavour — is given the chance to drive in an organised banger race. Although this involves an element of fun, the participants soon realise that the sport is highly competitive and quite dangerous, so it is very different from the driving they are used to. Their craving for excitement is therefore satisfied in a way that also makes them confront their fears and vulnerabilities.

A further practical benefit of the project is that it teaches the basic skills needed to pass the driving test. A collaboration between The National Association of Motor Projects, the British School of Motoring and the Sabre Insurance company has resulted in a scheme known as 'Fresh Start', which allows former project members who have not re-offended for at least six months to take an advanced driving course and obtain third party insurance at normal prices.

The majority of previous offenders leave the project as legal drivers and responsible citizens. It is surely no coincidence that during the 1990s the levels of theft of and from vehicles in Essex has fallen to well below the national average.

Birmingham Prison's Stepping Out programme

One of the reasons that so many convicted people re-offend is that their criminal record prevents them from gaining the steady employment necessary to support themselves and their families. This problem is especially acute for former prisoners, who often lack the composure and confidence to hold down a steady job.

Stepping Out is a unique programme, designed to help prisoners overcome these barriers. It began in 1996 following an event jointly organised by the Employment Service, the APEX Trust, and Marks and Spencer. It involves a partnership between the West Midlands Probation Service, Birmingham Prison, the Employment Service, and the city's Training and Enterprise and Economic Development Councils.

The programme aims to provide continuity of support after release from prison. Those nearing the end of their sentence participate in Stepping Out as part of a broader group work programme run by the prison. As well as offering a range of employment and training services, the programme helps to address basic problems, such as housing and drug and alcohol abuse, which often stand in the way of ex-prisoners finding employment. By the time they leave the prison, programme members will have an appointment with an employment resource centre, college, training agency or Job Link, but will continue to get guidance and support. The project has forged good connections with a number of local companies and during its first year, despite having only two workers, it was able to help 16 former prisoners into jobs, 25 into training, and gave guidance to a further 200.

Leeds Victim–Offender Unit

The Leeds Victim–Offender Unit was established in 1985, and was one of the first specialist probation teams in Britain to work with victims and offenders. It is entirely funded by the West Yorkshire Probation Service. An example of the Unit's work is taken from its most recent annual report,[4] and concerns two youths (aged 15) jointly charged with arson (having been caught setting fire to bales of hay in the barn of a farm smallholding). Of note, one of the boys had been in trouble before, and at the time of the offence both were playing truant from school.

Mediators visited the victim of the arson and the two youths separately, and all agreed to participate in the mediation process. This took the form of a meeting, a few days prior to the court hearing, held at a local community centre. Present at the meeting were two mediators, the victim, and the two offenders. The victim was able to convey directly to the offenders the full consequences of the fire, and her feelings about the crime. The boys had to listen, and through the mediation process became aware of the consequences of their actions. As a result both stressed that they would keep out of trouble, and apologised to the victim.

At court both boys were sentenced to 12 months' supervision, and each was ordered to pay £50 compensation. The court took into consideration the process of mediation in awarding this sentence, and both boys described the process as a 'difficult' but 'positive' experience. Just as importantly, the victim said that she felt very pleased with the process of mediation, which had exceeded her expectations and had restored her faith in the criminal justice system.

Between 1 April 1996 and 31 March 1997, the Victim–Offender Unit completed 106 mediation cases, of which only 7 per cent were, like the one described, face-to-face meetings. Of late there has been a move towards 'indirect mediation', which does not involve direct contact between the offender and the victim. The types of offences committed by those offenders who agreed to take part in the process ranged from arson and burglary, to theft and threats to kill.

In total there have been three reconviction studies carried out on the Leeds scheme — in 1988, 1992, and 1996. All show a clear benefit to offenders in terms of a lower rate of reconviction than expected after mediation took place. However, reconviction rates are only part of the story, as victims who engage in the mediation process indicate that they are 'satisfied' or 'very satisfied' with the outcome.

---

[4] West Yorkshire Probation Service, *Victim–Offender Unit, Annual Report, 1996/97*. All quotes and figures are taken from the Report.

PROBATION AND THE FUTURE

It is ironic, given all that we have described, that it is the probation service, more than any other agency within the criminal justice system, which has become a target for public and political disquiet about crime in our country. Probation is clearly no soft option, despite what we are told by the Press. A strong probation service has to be central to any rational and cost-effective approach to combatting crime, and as such it is likely to become more directly concerned with crime prevention in the future. In doing so it will undoubtedly develop closer working relationships with a variety of other agencies within the criminal justice system, but we hope that it plays the lead role within that relationship rather than becoming the poor relation.

Given the growing indication that the prison service and the probation service will work more closely together, perhaps it is worth considering each agency's contribution in combatting crime, as a means of establishing priorities for any new 'Corrections Service'. In doing so we do not want to promote competition between the two services, but rather to establish some guidelines for any new partnership. We have chosen the following factors to make such a comparison:

- value for money
- rehabilitation
- effectiveness in reducing reconvictions.

It is clear, using current figures, that the average cost of imprisonment is 10 times that of a community service order or probation order. This calculation is merely based on the costs of the sentence itself. As we have indicated elsewhere, financial resources are required to support a prisoner's family. Someone on probation, on the other hand, is still able to work, and thus able to make financial contributions in the form of tax. Prison compares poorly with the probation service in providing programmes which combat these factors. The former, for example, usually targets programmes dealing with anti-social attitudes and behaviours of high-risk prisoners, who are assessed as being capable of responding to this form of intervention, whereas the probation service delivers these programmes to a much wider audience. Similarly, over 90 per cent of prisoners released from prison in 1996 were unemployed and had no immediate job prospects. The probation service again seems to have been better able to respond to this factor in an offender's profile.

Prisoners are offered help and advice about drugs and alcohol. We have already drawn attention to the calamatous effects of the prison service's mandatory drug treatment programme, which seems to encourage prisoners to switch from 'soft' to 'hard' drugs. In short, drugs remain a widespread problem inside our prisons, no matter the good intentions of prison staff. By way of contrast, the annual statistics of most probation areas show significant improvements in relation to drug and alcohol dependency, as a result of supervision in the community.

Lastly, we have already drawn attention to a variety of research demonstrating the effectiveness of probation in relation to its impact on reconviction. Perhaps more than any other factor, the ability of the probation service to get people to stop committing crime has to be seen as its major contribution in creating a safer Britain. Prisons might always be necessary so as to protect our community from very dangerous and harmful offenders, but the vast majority of offenders are not like that. Consequently, we should target our resources based on the evidence of who is committing crime, why, and what is likely to help them make a positive contribution within our community. In all these respects it is probation rather than prison which offers most of the answers.

A Vision for the Future

This book stemmed from frustration. A frustration which has seen crime, and the fear of crime, gradually increase over the past two decades, despite the massive amount of taxpayers' money spent on the various agencies of the criminal justice system. This frustration has become more difficult to bear as 'Law and Order' — like employment, the economy, and inflation — has become a political football, with each party trying to outscore the other. All too often all we have been left with is a series of own goals ... And now we have New Labour.

It is difficult not to feel some sympathy for New Labour: many of the problems which they've inherited were not of their own making; and we sense a desire to 'do good by stealth', as the incoming Home Affairs team explained to the Prison Reform Trust. However, that really is not good enough, and we naïvely expect our politicians to be at the forefront of this debate, attempting to create the news rather than respond to the next media panic. On the other hand, New Labour also reap what they have sown. After all, Jack Straw supported the Crime (Sentences) Act, which has introduced mandatory minimum sentences, initially in an effort to neutralise the Conservatives on law and order; but his new flagship legislation — The Crime and Disorder Bill — is in reality very similar to what might have been enacted by his predecessor. In short, it is 'business as usual' at the Home Office.

In an effort to prompt some debate in this overheated area of public policy, we have attempted to show how we have got ourselves into the position which we are currently in, and to suggest ways out. In particular we have drawn attention to examples of 'best practice' in the probation service, in our prisons, and in our schools. If we were to adopt this 'best practice' throughout the criminal justice system, we would make a dramatic impact on crime in our country, and also go a long way to eradicating some of the racism within the agencies which make up that system. More importantly, we have tried to draw attention to the fact that if we are serious about fighting crime, most if not all of the solutions rarely lie within the criminal justice system. In this respect we have spent some time explaining the failures of our police force.

In doing all of this we have attempted to describe the realities of who actually commits crime, and the circumstances that encourage crime to flourish. These realities might not sell newspapers, or make good TV, but they are nonetheless true. In particular we have drawn attention to the difficulties faced by our young people — both girls and boys — as they attempt to make their way in the world. We have shown that there really isn't a readily identifiable group of 'persistent' young offenders committing the vast majority of crime in our country, and that crimes such as the murder of James Bulger, whilst horrific, are extremely unusual. Consequently, we have argued against many of the provisions of the Crime and Disorder Bill, and the use of secure training centres. The only people to profit from these institutions will be the private companies who win the contracts to run them.

We have also taken some time to outline a case for a more progressive view about drugs. As the Home Secretary himself has discovered, the use of cannabis in this country is widespread, and will remain so despite 'parental responsibility orders'. However, we are also aware of the damage done by drugs — especially heroin — and have used the latest research to demonstrate how other countries have dealt with this problem beyond criminalisation. The result has been a dramatic fall in street crime, especially robbery.

Much of this book has focused on the experiences of the United States of America. This is inevitable given that successive Home Office teams seem to have found their inspiration on the other side of the Atlantic. Boot camps, zero tolerance and mandatory minimum sentences are only the most obvious examples of this process. We have drawn attention to where these types of policies have led in America, with its vast prison population and equally vast expenditure on the 'penal – industrial complex'. None of these policies has made the United States any safer, and their murder rate, for example, remains seven times greater than our own.

Lastly, as our description of developments in France and Switzerland might have indicated, we would encourage any new Home Office team to set their sights across the Channel, rather than on the other side of the Atlantic. Our nearest European neighbour, for example, responding to riots in the ghetto suburbs of Lyons and Marseilles in 1981, adopted initiatives which forged links between the situational, political, and social dimensions of crime prevention, as well as creating a link between youth crime and youth justice. This resulted in the development of local, informal groups of young people, politicians, residents and local government officials, who would meet as a community to discuss strategies for crime prevention and intervention. These groups were typically chaired by the Mayor, who in turn sat on a national crime prevention committee, chaired by the deputy Prime Minister. The result was the development of significant social programmes in high-crime neighbourhoods, whereby, for example, rather than getting offenders into treatment programmes or put in prison, they were helped to find decent accommodation, sort out their financial affairs, given help with their addictions, and in doing so were able to develop, or sustain, a secure relationship with another person. All of this has made a significant impact on the French crime rate. In 1981, recorded crime in both France and England and Wales stood at 3,500,000. By the end of the decade French recorded crime had dropped to 3,000,000 while in England and Wales it had increased to 5,500,000. It is also significant that the greatest increases in our own country tended to be in the poorest communities, whereas in France it was these areas where the falls in crime were at their most dramatic.

Of course, by 1981 we had elected a government which denied that there was any link between crime and the social circumstances in which people found themselves, or that the state should intervene in society to ameliorate those circumstances. Indeed, the Government even denied the existence of 'society'. It is all too obvious that 'society' exists, and we hope that this book has gone some way to explaining why New Labour should follow the French example, rather than the American. Any anti-crime strategy has got to involve the community, rather than merely being concerned with its policing. Perhaps then New Labour really will be able to deliver on the second half of the Prime Minister's famous sound bite. By concentrating more on being 'tough on the causes of crime', we might just be able to make our country safer.

Appendix

Committee members of *What Everyone in Britain should know about Crime and Punishment*:

Colin Allen, HM Deputy Chief Inspector of Prisons
Pauline Austin, The New Bridge
Farida Anderson, POPS
Shane Bryans, Prison Governor
Sarah Bucknill, Teacher
Kate Cawley, Prison Governor
Bob Colover, Barrister
Claire Holden, Criminologist
Peter Jones, Senior Probation Officer
Jerry Knight, Prison Governor
Sir Peter Lloyd, Politician
Eugene McLaughlin, Criminologist
Jenny Roberts, Chief Probation Officer
Paul Roberts, Teacher
Doug Sharp, Criminologist
Richard Sparks, Criminologist
Paddy Tomkins, Police Commander
Jackie Worrall, NACRO

Index